The Outside Girl

a memoir by Jade Mari

Visit Jade at jademari.com

First edition

ISBN (paperback): 979-8-9927565-0-0
ISBN (hardcover): 979-8-9927565-1-7

Cover art by Eric Tyler
Editing by Katie DeShane
Advising by Kaylin Kustura

For my children—
You saved me just by being.
Thank you for choosing me as your mother.

Contents

Foreword   iii

Preface   iv

I   Childhood

1   Shepherds, Hippies, and My Mama   3
2   The Baptists, Mennonites, and Scary Teachers   10
    To the Outside Girl, with Love   20

II   Teen Years

3   Baby *Suddenly* Got Back   23
4   It's Goin' Down for Reals   32
    To the Outside Girl, with Love   43

III   The Reaping

5   How to Fake It 'Til You Make It   47
6   Mr. Callihan   54
    To the Outside Girl, with Love   62

IV   Adulting

7   If You Can't Be With the One You Love, Honey, Love
    the One...   65

8 Lessons in Love   77
To the Outside Girl, with Love   93

V   Pluto Square Pluto

9 The Quickening   97
10 I Will Not Go Gently Into That Good Night   110
To the Outside Girl, with Love   123

VI   How to Begin Again

11 An Adultress and an Addict Walk Into a Gym…   127
12 Desire Is Your Own Want   138
To the Outside Girl, with Love   148

VII   It Ain't Over 'Til It's Over

13 WTF   151
14 Operation Re-Parent Self   162
To the Outside Girl, with Love   169

Afterword   170
A Sample of Eric's Poetry   171
  Portrait   171
  Breathe   172
  All Within A Breath   173
Acknowledgments   174
About the Author   175

Foreword

A Note to the Reader,

At the end of every section, you'll find a passage titled, *To the Outside Girl, with Love.* These words came from a place I can only describe as The Voice: something deeper and wiser than my conscious mind. It's source, Love herself, speaking back to me.

This practice, inspired by the lovely Elizabeth Gilbert, is something I do often, usually with my eyes closed, letting the words come through me, not from me. If the rest of the memoir is my attempt to make sense of my past, these letters are the part that always knew the truth.

Consider them love notes from the inside out.

Preface

This memoir is a personal account of my life experiences, told from my perspective. While I have taken care to recall events as accurately as possible, memory is subjective, and others may remember these events differently. This book reflects my truth, as I experienced and understood it.

To protect the privacy of certain individuals, I have changed names and altered identifying details where appropriate. However, when individuals in positions of power or authority have misused that power to harm, abuse, or exploit vulnerable people, I have chosen to name them and recount events with as much detail and truth as humanly possible. Additionally, some names—whether of beloved family members or others—have not been changed because it was either not possible to do so without compromising the integrity of the story or because I chose to preserve the authenticity of those relationships and events.

Readers should understand that this memoir includes sensitive topics, including abuse and trauma. While difficult, these truths are part of my journey and essential to the narrative I've chosen to share.

I recognize that people mentioned in this memoir may have their own versions of events, and I do not claim to speak for anyone but myself. My intention is not to cause harm but to tell my story with honesty and integrity.

I

Childhood

"Be happy for no reason, like a child. If you are happy for a reason you are in trouble, because that reason can be taken from you." - Deepak Chopra

1

Shepherds, Hippies, and My Mama

The step stool has made me just the right height, and now I can see perfectly into the black enamel pot with little white specks, full of a dark, slippery mess of pureed plums. My mother's face is rueful, amused, but she's not angry.

"I give up. That's not going to set... what a waste." She says some more fretful words, though with a smile, and then, "Do you want to make something with this?"

Ummm, do I ever. The tall canning pot isn't daunting to me, nor is the tangy plum substance inside. I'm full of inspiration. My mother hands me the long-handled spoon, suggests some spices from the cupboard, and goes to take a bath.

For the next 30 minutes I pull out spices and add honey: cloves, ginger, cinnamon, cardamom, and keep sniffing and tasting. I can hear her sloshing in the tub and don't even think to wash the spoon between tastes. I don't pause once or worry it won't work. I just know it will, and the failed jam moves from tangy and bitter to spicy and slightly sweet.

Sometime during this process my mother has come out of the bathroom and watches me finish, only coming to taste when I say it's ready. She tastes it and I see true surprise on her face because it's genuinely delicious. We jar up every ounce, she sets the jars in a boiling water bath to properly can them, and labels the jars "Plum Sauce." That sauce would go on to last for years and was especially delicious on her homemade yogurt.

That's a good memory from when I was seven years old. Everything in my childhood can be placed into two compartments: before my sister Mary was born, ages 1-5, and before my mother married and we moved, ages 5-12.

I'm going back now to Before Mary, memories I shouldn't be able to recall so clearly, but certain moments stand out in sharp relief. With the wisdom of time I'm able to see that my perspective is just that, but my version of events can come instantaneously and play like a movie I've seen over and over, or in the form of a perfume that smells like sadness.

I am young in these memories so they feel like an adventure. I'm not so sure about the Ponytail Man, but he is friendly enough. My mother's hand is warm and strong and she carries me when I need her. Ponytail Man strides ahead, and looks back with white teeth gleaming through his beard in a smile.

"Hold out your thumb, like this!" he tells me. My mom giggles nervously and tugs my small arm out as straight as it can go. She shows me with her own arm and hand how to thumbs up.

"This is the best way to get a ride," he says. "We'll go in style. We're not walking to Washington!"

Washington is all trees: trees and forests and apples. There is a cabin in the woods full of people. It is a revolving door of dogs, cats, and people coming in and out to stand by the fire or eat from the table. I cry a little when a woman with a kerchief continuously sprinkles brewer's yeast on my food, but when I can't find my mother in the warm crush of bodies, I am wracked with sobs. The woman *tsks* at me. She picks me up and sets me with the other children. I am inconsolable and utterly terrified. By the time my mom finally comes back to me, the adventure is ruined. There is no more safety in my body, no more excitement over new things.

I don't remember how we make it back to Idaho, only that the Ponytail Man is a shepherd. He shepherds his flock in a field dotted with covered wagons; he has his own wagon with one bed and sometimes my mother and I sleep with him there. I make my body small in the corner: there is fear in the smell of sex, but also power and excitement.

I decide that sheep are stupid. I don't like them at all. They smell like a lot and their eyes are empty when they all run together. Their wool is dirty, and once men grab the sheep's legs and shave it off, it has to be picked until your fingers are raw, and carded with combs, and it takes too long and I get bored. Gross.

It's not all bad. I do like the smell of Castille peppermint soap. It will always smell like hot springs to me. I love the mineral-y water and even the name makes me happy: Banbury Hot Springs. The springs are a place where we can have our own cave of water sectioned off for privacy and we get naked and free. Maybe too free? Ponytail Man lifts my mother onto him even when I am there. I'm not watching really, but I'm certainly present. The sex and power of Ponytail Man feels like fear and excitement to my mother. I understand this in the core of my being and will take it on as my own.

There is a time when Ponytail Man takes my mother to his small, narrow house on wheels. My mama always has me in tow, so naturally he takes my mother *and* me to his house. When we walk in there is a sad, pretty woman with long hair and many children around her, all sitting at a table. Ponytail Man kisses the woman on top of her head and leads my mother down the dark hallway, telling me with his eyes I am not to follow. I wait quietly on the brown couch and stay frozen in my body until my mom comes back to me.

I have many grandmas in my life: two of my mom's grandmas and grandmas of my cousins, but Grandma Abshire is my best grandma. Even though she's very busy with all of the people she still gives my mom a break and I stay with her and all her other children, my aunts and uncles. They are mostly grown ups but they're always in and out of the house, and they have some children of their own who are my cousins, but I'm the oldest of the cousins and feel most special.

The house is smooshed with bodies but I don't mind. My grandma lets me watch all the good shows like Daisy Duke in her short shorts. There are four rooms in Grandma's house: one room has a couch that fits four people and everyone else is on the floor, one bedroom is for my grandma and grandpa (whose snores rumble through the whole house), and one bedroom is for the six kids, but there are only two kids left for the most part. There's one bathroom but DON'T FLUSH THE TOILET PAPER FOR GOD'S SAKE. There's one washing machine in the bathroom and all the clothes hang on the line outside. In winter they freeze dry but my grandma says it's no problem. She makes the best biscuits and bacon and eggs with pepper. My grandpa puts on even more pepper. At night he sets up a sleeve of saltine crackers, a jar of chunky Jif, a knife, and a bear of honey. It's a cycle of knife into peanut butter, peanut butter to cracker, a squeeze of the bear, and it all goes into his mouth in one bite, his mustache moving up and down until the sleeve is gone.

The barn is my favorite place. It's full of feral kittens you can sometimes see but hardly ever touch. In one room there's tall bins of oats and corn and grain. My grandma complains that she "just cannot understand how the mice get in!" So you have to be careful when you open the lid to the dried goods. I always eat some of the oats and corn before we fill up an old coffee can to call the horses to us. I even sneak a lick on the salt blocks.

I like the hen house and getting the eggs with my grandma in the mornings; I like the cluck cluck and the rickety door. The tackle barn is next to the hen house and I can see the horse blankets and smell the saddle oil. The roosters have their own pens; they are beautiful but dangerous. If they're out for exercise they'll attack. My grandpa laughs and says that's what they're made for. He says you have to let roosters face off because that's what they like best. He has a lot of roosters and feeds them the finest food until they shine so people will bet on his roosters to win when they fight in a dusty ring with the spikey spurs he keeps for their legs. And gol-dammit, he usually does win.

There are dogs on the farm too, but "Bull Dog" is the only name they're all given. My grandpa is always shouting, "Bull Dog, lay down!" The dog never does. It chases the roosters, gets in trouble, and gets hit by the cars right outside the house, and then there's a new dog.

Someone helps me climb up the side of the wall ladder of the barn and hang on to the rope. The attic is up there, usually with an owl blinking and observing, and my grandpa's old chariot he used to win races with. In the pictures with the chariot and horses, he looks like a movie star in his cowboy hat and boots. It smells like dust and corn and horses, the best smell in the world. Laying my head down and pressing my nose against a hot horse while it snickers becomes home to me. I just want to be on a horse's back. I am content to walk or trot, but galloping is the best; nothing beats that flying feeling.

One day, Grandpa puts me on crazy Pinto the Paint but she immediately bucks me off and smashes my fingers. He roped that horse in the wild, brought her home, and trained her, so he is not impressed with me. Another day, I'm playing with my pet goat like always when she suddenly stops liking me and hits me with her horns over and over. I'm pretty sure she's trying to kill me so I scream and cry, but my grandpa just watches and tells me to move out of the way. I can't because I am frozen with fear, so I just keep screaming. My mama runs to me from the house, kicking that naughty goat as she lifts me high. My grandpa shakes his head at both of us. My mom says he thinks we're "dramatic" but we both know that was a close call.

The outside of the little smooshed house goes on forever. There's a creek but DON'T GO DOWN BY THE CREEK FOR GOD'S SAKE, and a pasture full of horses. My uncles and Grandpa are always moving tarps attached to long boards to water the pastures and grow the grass. There's a ditch in front of the house and that one is safe for swimming, but you have to check for leeches on your skin when you're finished.

When my mom comes to pick me up in our blue Chevy pickup, she always brings me a can of grape Crush. I drink it on her lap and my grandma says, "Niecey, you spoil her rotten!" She says it with a smile and a wink because she spoils me rotten too. I feel like that's the right thing to do.

I bounce out to the truck with glee, happy to be reunited with my mom and excited to ride in the truck. We're all very proud of it because my grandpa gave it to us. "It's a 1951 Chevy and it still runs just fine!" he assures us. I like it because there's no seatbelts and sometimes I get to ride in the back if I'm sitting on my bottom and holding on to the side.

We never know what we might do on the way home. My mama has good rules, like don't peek in people's houses unless they have their curtains open or we're absolutely sure it's empty, and always, *always* have your eyes peeled

7

for great things on the side of the road.

One day, we're driving through the country and we spy with our little eyes some fresh asparagus growing outside a farm fence, sprouting up right by an irrigation ditch. My mom whoops with glee and we get out to pick it for our supper. There's an even bigger patch just barely on the other side of the fence. We can't pass that up, so my mom makes herself flat and squeezes the top part of her body under the fence, reaching out for the tender spears. Suddenly there's a loud pop-boom sound. We are both startled and look up from our positions on the ground to see an angry farmer shooting his gun. It's pointed in the air but you never know where he'll point it next, so we screech and scurry back to the Chevy pickup. My mama doesn't drop the asparagus though.

I'm around a lot of different kinds of people, and the frozen feeling is happening in my body more and more but I don't feel afraid. It makes it so that sometimes things are happening to me that I'm not even conscious of until I hear my mother's voice or see her face. There's one night that there are lots of men in our house and my mom is in the bedroom but I'm not scared for some reason. When she comes out she calls my name. Her voice sounds surprised and fearful, and I look around to realize I'm very comfy on a man's lap playing with his earlobe. It's big and hang-y and I'm laid out across his lap watching it swing when I flick it gently with my finger. He says he doesn't mind and I believe him. I don't mind it either, but my mom sure does.

We spend a lot of time at a group of cabins. I love a woman there named Susannah and her son Nathan. He has brown eyes and blonde curls. He's big like me, but he can still have his mama in his mouth. That must be nice. Susannah's cabin is covered in ropes of garlic hanging from the rafters. There is always a pot of something cooking at the fire and Nathan is attached to her at all times.

I love the dusty trails of the compound. You can walk around barefoot with kittens mewling beside you and the dust covers you in yellow powder on your way to see Bill in the back pasture. Bill doesn't seem to belong to anyone but he knows a lot about plants. He lives in a teepee and doesn't appreciate being interrupted so we tiptoe close and hope for an invitation.

One day I see Bill and my mom in a back room of a cabin and he is touching her round stomach. I am shooed away but this time it's fine; I don't have the frozen feeling or smell the sex, which means my mom feels safe, so I can feel safe in my body too. He comes out and shouts happily, "It's going to be a boy!" but I peer into the empty room and don't see any boys. I shrug and move along.

Dan and Peggy are also comforting to me. Their daughter, Arianna, is my good friend. I like to spend the night with them the best. Dan, the dad, is kind. Peggy, the mom, lets me have pink frosting. I accidentally see Dan the dad's bare bum and long penis once because he hears something outside late at night and comes to investigate. He thinks I'm asleep but I'm definitely not. He is very naked but not worried about anyone seeing. Interesting.

I'm very excited one night because we're going to Dan and Peggy's. We're going to stay with them for a while and I know I will get to play with Arianna and see Peggy's pretty face and have a good time. I wait for my mom in our pickup with excitement. She had to hurry into the post office just before it closes. I'm in the front seat, so I can see when she runs back out the door and down the steps toward me. She's unusually fast and breathless when she gets in the truck.

My whole night changes in an instant. I cry and even scream a little because suddenly we can't go to Peggy and Dan's anymore. Now I have to go to my grandma's and my mom has to go to the hospital. Apparently that boy Bill was talking about has been in her stomach all this time and wants to come out because some water broke, "RIGHT IN THE POST OFFICE!" I don't know what all that means, but I'm mad.

2

The Baptists, Mennonites, and Scary Teachers

It's Christmas morning and Santa has eaten the cookies. There's just crumbs left which I think is so exciting. I don't care that we don't have a chimney and Santa is probably not real, I just like the crumbs on the plate and the empty glass. I'm happy to pretend when it makes me shivery. I get the same feeling when we run out of gas, lock ourselves out of the house, or go down Black Bear Hill in the old Chevy "on a wing and a prayer"; I can turn the adventures into floppy shivers in my tummy.

I gasp when I look under the tree. There are two blue and white nightgowns that look exactly the same. The biggest one for me, because I'm five years older than Mary. Hers is tiny and she puts it on and dances around the living room, petting its softness with her hands. Mary was not a boy after all, but a girl with rosy cheeks and big blue eyes. My mother and I take care of her and we are all pretty dang happy together. Mary is just precious in general, like when she makes us laugh until we cry while she plays with the knobs on the stereo. She knows she's not supposed to, but she turns her head and stares at us with her giant blue eyes full of innocence, truly believing we can't see her being naughty because she can't see herself.

I am very aware that we don't ever have enough money because my mom says it out loud a lot. The buzzy, scared feeling that comes from her translates directly to me. Even as we open our gifts she frets because it might not be enough, and she tells us how she paid the old neighbor lady down the street to sew our nightgowns and crochet our Barbies' new clothes; slim skirts, a tiny beret, and dresses with layers and flounces. But she frets with a smile and her eyes are shiny because we're so happy with the beautiful new things.

It's 1983 and I'm eight years old. I think I could be happy to stay cocooned with just my mother and my sister in an endless summer for the rest of my childhood. Now that Mary is here, my mom is home a lot more and there's no more men or loud people in the house, which is just fine with me. But cocoons are not meant to be forever homes I guess.

I am a terrific, and I mean truly fantastic, skater. I'm always on my skates, or cooking without fire outside, or sweeping out my shed house and making its cot bed. Our tiny white house comes with a landlord (we don't care for him) but used to be owned by old people who created a koi fish pond and "landscaped" the area. They also built an outdoor oven and grill out of brick. The pond is a dried up hole and covered with bushes, the chimney of the oven is cracked and crumbly, and there are black widow spiders in the house-shed, but it's paradise to me. In the summer, I read books in the branches of our old swinging oak tree in the front yard, skate to the neighbor's, and play house all day every day.

One night I come in just as darkness begins to fall, my mother's unspoken rule for when to be home. I am full of bliss and breathless with the joy of being an outside girl. The living room is dim, practically dark, and I see with my eyes that my mother is not alone. More so than my eyes, my goosebumps, prickly hairs on my neck, and sick feeling in my stomach warn me of danger.

My mother's voice is soft and small. "Jade, you remember Jonathan don't you?" It's Ponytail Man, and just like that, the freezing feeling is back. I am completely frozen in my body but my strong skater legs and my joy want to fight it off, so I scream.

From this point forward, when my mom brings a man into the house, I scream and kick and cry. My aunts and grandma try to intervene and *tsk* me into polite behavior, but I will have none of it and continue to throw temper tantrums for years. It's all out of my control at this point.

11

It's not just the men. Sometimes other people coming into the house makes me crazy too. One night my friend Betsy looks at my mom with an intense shine in her eyes and asks to stay for dinner. All of a sudden, I can't stand having her in the house any longer and she gets some good screams too. Screaming and hatefulness chase away the frozen feelings. I am now a fighter.

My best friend is a little, curly black dog that belongs to the neighbors, but follows me around the neighborhood gazing at me adoringly. For that reason, and because she's soft and warm and can lick my tears away when I'm sad and listens to me sing all my best songs, I let her follow me around all day. On my birthday, the neighbors give me a big box that's shaking and moving. Out pops my curly best friend - she's mine all mine! My mom is not thrilled about this, but no one can stop our love.

Later that night, she's cutting corn off the cob and putting it into baggies for the freezer when she asks me what I will name the black dog. She says it should be something better than "the dog."

Hmmm, I think.

"Why are you putting that corn into the freezer?" I ask, distracted.

"To keep it fresh," she answers.

I ponder that for a minute and move the word around in my mouth. I like it.

The dog's name is Fresh. She doesn't need a leash or a fence. She comes when you go outside and shout "HERRRREEE FRESHHH!" You have to drag out the words and make it nice and loud, but she's never far away and comes running straight into your arms with a dog-smile. She's a bundle of joy.

Let's get right to the point: we are Baptists. We used to be hippies, but now, pretty much since Mary was born, we have become Southern Baptists who go to church at least three times a week. We don't see Susannah, or Bill, or Dan and Peggy anymore. Now we've fallen in with the Kimberlys who met us in a park and invited us to church. They have three little girls, but Jodi is my favorite because we like the same things. She has long hair like me, and glasses that make her eyes big and shiny when she looks at me.

Mrs. Kimberly likes to pretend that raw beet milk tastes like chocolate milk, so now we do too. No more white things like white flour, fluffy rice, and sugar. No chocolate, just carob, and only organic things. I hate dinner so much it makes me full of sadness. I can't fight my mother on this. I have to console myself with some of the little things I do, like putting my plum sauce on her homemade yogurt and her granola (so good she labels it "Janice's Granola" and sells it in the co-op), fresh ground peanut butter and raw honey on rice cakes, and milk in a gallon jar, still warm from the cow. The cream at the top adds so much extra flavor. My mom says it's "too rich" but ladles some on my oatmeal and turns the rest into butter. We are never sick and my mom knows it's because she's close to God now, and helping us honor our temples with good food.

Some of the fight has gone out of me. There's just too much kicking to be done, even for my strong skater legs. I try for years to have joy and fun in school, but it doesn't work one bit. In Kindergarten, my old woman teacher yells and gets sweaty because I can't make my name look nice. I try to care, I really do.

One day at school I am surprised and delighted to be the chosen one to go outside the classroom door and put the attendance card in the little pocket. I can barely reach it but it slides in so nicely. I think it would be more fun to take the cards out, rather than put them in, and collecting these cards is a job I can do very well. I see rows of cards outside all the classrooms and my heart is thrilled. I will show everyone what a good collector looks like. I make it all the way upstairs to the 5th grade classrooms, and have not missed one single card, but then a teacher with squinty eyes pokes her head out of her classroom and says, "Just what do you think you're doing?" She grabs my arm in a pinchy way and asks everyone we pass in the hall where I "belong." It doesn't seem like anyone is happy with me. I am confused. I was working so hard.

Eventually, my mom decides I need even MORE God, so in 2nd and 3rd grade I go to a school that is beyond strange. Every student wears the same, scratchy clothes. We sit in cubicles facing the wall with little holes above them where we stick tiny American and Christian flags when we need help. The American flag calls over the Superintendent-man-in-charge, and the

13

Christian flag brings a woman teacher.

They promise to help me with math. Math is the scariest thing in the world to me. I try to pretend it's not there, but every day, there it is again. We sit all day and do our work, then we grade it ourselves at big tables. One day I'm grading my math test with terror and feel a hot trickling down my legs. I'm so afraid of math I've peed my pants over it.

It costs a lot of money for this strange school, and one day someone brings cake from the store for their birthday. I sneak an extra piece, but then I'm sick for three days. My mom is not pleased with the direction I'm headed in, so it's back to the public school for me.

While I've been gone, all my friends have new friends, so I don't have anyone anymore. I feel like I'm a strange girl. My clothes don't look like everyone else's. It's too bad there are no more uniforms, because I only have a few pairs of pants, which Julie the Rich Girl points out to everyone.

Now I am in Ms. Juker's class. She was the teacher with squinty eyes that pinched my arm when I was in Kindergarten and I want her to like me, but unfortunately she does not. It's Ritchie the Outcast with Asthma and me. We are on the same team, and it is not a winning one. We get teased and bullied and no one ever gets in trouble. Ms. Juker herself makes fun of me because I don't understand things. She slaps my math tests down and screams the bad grade to everyone. She looks at me like she wants me to be dead.

At lunchtime, my rice cakes and peanut butter don't match everyone's bologna sandwiches, so I sit with Ritchie and wait for him to finish his lunch. He almost always lets me have his Hostess pie. The blackberry is my favorite.

I know part of the problem: I can't stop being shiny. My hair is very long and shiny, for example. All the adults touch it and talk about its many colors of gold and caramel. My SELF is shiny. I can read big, thick books in hours. It is so easy for me to read that it's all I want to do. Julie the Rich Girl hates me but is also fascinated by me, mostly because her boyfriend stares at me like he's enchanted. Julie brings me her big sister's romance novels and watches me read them so fast, watches me sneak them into my textbook and then rats me out, watches me go from the star reading group where all the smart kids are to the bottom math group with all the rejects, always constantly watching me. I'm the only one who is in both groups. I seem to confuse everybody. I can't help but stand out.

I don't try very hard to make people like me in the classroom, but sometimes I create games on the playground and get all the grades involved. I start a crack-the-whip chain and make everyone pause while I count how many people I collect: 62. I make up a game where one person is selected to be the shopper in a robot shop. What do they most need and want in their robot today?! Everyone is a robot, frozen, and the shop owner, the conductor of the game, (always me) directs the shopper to their "button." Then the robots have to turn on, trying not to laugh if their button was their ribs or armpit, and act out something special and funny enough to make the shopper choose them, then they get to be the shopper. Everyone loves that game; it's a great one. I'm so clever.

At home, God and Jesus are front and center of our lives. I sing at our church in front of everyone and my pastor gives me a certificate that says "Cream of the Crop." If I'm being honest, I don't like church much at all, but I do very much like the babies in the nursery. I'm the helper almost every week after Sunday School.

One day I go in and the adults aren't there yet, but the moms and dads leave all the children with me anyway because I've got it under control until the real help arrives. The only tiny problem is that the adults never show up and now I'm stuck with a few babies and several small-ish children by myself. I definitely put a diaper on one of them backwards, not my favorite part of the job, but I'm certain I can take care of these rascals all by myself. I'm ten years old after all. And I do. There's mostly wonder, and only some dismay when the parents come back. I am flushed with victory.

Many events take place on the streets around that Baptist church. One night we're on a family walk in the dark, my favorite kind of walk, just the three of us wrapped in the quiet blanket of night. Fresh is trotting ahead and we spy a cat lurking in the shadows ahead of us. Fresh's best-loved game is Go Get That Kitty Cat, where she chases any kitty even though she knows she'll never catch it, because that's not the point. When we spy the cat, we say it to her in just the right way, "Fresh! Go Get That Kitty Cat!!" and off she goes. This time, when she reaches the cat she lets out a whimper, puts her tail between her legs, and runs back to us before the game is over. We all shriek at the same time because that cat? That cat is actually a sewer rat. Here in Idaho, rats and Jack-rabbits are of the large variety. Poor Fresh.

Another time, the ol' Chevy is making the wrong kind of noises on the way home from errands, which is nothing new, but just to be safe my mama makes me get out to stand on the side of the road while she figures it out. I'm walking in front of the truck when I feel a whispery wind and hear a zzzzzz sound. A fan blade had ripped right through the metal of the hood, whipped straight past my soft skull, and landed several houses away.

My mom starts screaming as she jumps from the truck and runs towards me. "Jade! Jade! Are you okay?!"

I am perfectly fine but have now had my second brush with death. The first was back when I was a tiny baby and I fell off the bike my mom was riding while holding me, so I don't remember it, but my mom had to tell me the story because I have a scar on my forehead to prove it. I am in shock, but I will remember this near-death experience. Our pickup has a scar for the rest of its life, just like me.

My mama was the only one of her siblings to get more education after high school. She had become a nurse before Mary was born and needs someone to watch us while she works the summers. Of course, she needs someone who loves God and Jesus A LOT and will keep us safe from the many dangers of the world, so she chooses Mennonites.

Now, if you've never heard about Mennonites let me tell you, because I have practically lived with them. They are easy to spot: the women wear the same dress pattern in different fabrics, but it always has flowers. They do not cut their hair ever, but wind it in buns and pin it under black caps on their heads. The men have beards, and button down shirts with belts or suspenders. They have their own schools that stop after 8th grade so the children can help their parents farm. A few select children can keep going to school and even college so they can have doctors and lawyers and nurses in their community. They have cars and tractors, but all the radios are cut out. There are no TVs, but I'm used to that, because we don't really have one either. The rabbit ears we have never work.

In their churches, the men sit on one side, the women on the other, and there are no instruments allowed, only a mouthpiece to find the right note to start the hymn. When we go swimming, the girls have to wait for the boys to finish before we can take a turn. I feel the injustice of that deep in my bones. Their houses are nice and rich looking, their farms are huge, and most importantly, they make the best food from scratch I've ever tasted in my life. They use plenty of white stuff but also the best produce from their gardens and pots, so my mom can't say a word about it.

The Mennonites my mom has chosen to watch over Mary and me are dairy farmers with five boys. There are hundreds of cows being milked by machines twice a day and the whole operation smells like cool, clean, stone and cream. I find it fascinating, but they do not know what to do with me. I am chaotic and loud to them. When I'm not being loud, I'm sitting in the nice living room for hours and hours reading. I do not help the mother and I am not polite, but I am full of questions and challenges.

Mary, being so much smaller and simply precious, captures the mother's heart and she offers to adopt Mary, but not me. My mom is offended, and says that offer has been made for me a few times back in the day. It's because my mom was still in high school when she had me, and there's no dad for me or for Mary.

But no one wants to take me nowadays. I am a wild child. I like to flirt with all the boys of the family and sneak them scandalous stories about the county fair while they work. When they're not working, they have time to play and we build an almost real house with 2x4s. These boys know how to use hammers and nails and measure and plan - amazing!

One day I spy an old hay elevator in the back field, rickety and rusted over time. It's as tall as the Mennonites' big, nice house and I get an idea for a new game: we turn that hay elevator into a giant teeter-totter. Only one person gets to go up because it takes the weight of all the rest of us to make the other side go down, but I think it's even more thrilling than a fair ride, and I tell the boys exactly that so they'll keep sending me up into the sky with the wind in my hair and the sun on my face.

17

The summer is at an end and just in time. Both Mary and I have had enough of the Mennonites. Mary isn't as precious to them anymore after she decides to play hide-and-go-seek with the mom, but never comes out of her hiding place (she is incredible at hiding, it's true). We look for Mary for hours, calling for her over and over, all of us more frantic by the minute. Just when we decide to call the police to start a search and rescue, Mary comes out of her hiding place, *ta da*! I laugh and laugh but no one else is amused.

At the same time, the creepy oldest brother, Greg, who is basically a man, keeps trapping me in the basement. The frozen feeling is back in my body when I think about him, but I don't have anything to pull from my memory bank except that I escaped that house just in time, I think.

I'm too old for temper tantrums now so I just have to deal with things. For instance, my mom meets a foreigner. He is a Peruvian shepherd who wants to marry my mom and take us all back to his homeland. He tries to win me over with a tiny llama made of real llama hair and a woven blanket on its back. It is extremely adorable and I almost fall for it, but then he ruins it by bringing us mutton for dinner, which makes me puke in my mouth, and says, "Pass the honey, honey," to my mother at the dinner table, which also makes me puke in my mouth. I cry and beg her to leave him, but I do not scream this time and she listens to me. Crisis averted.

But I cannot stop the barreling freight train of David the forest firefighter. He is the brother and uncle of a family in our church, the Fuehrers, who are very cool because they raise turkeys, can raspberry jam, and have two boys for Mary and I to play with. Jason and Alex are annoying but I have fun with them. The mother, Anne, is very kind and loving and even lets Mary do Kindergarten with her son Alex, because Mary cried so hard when she went to school my mom didn't know what else to do. Mary knows when to put her little foot down.

So now my mom is in love with Anne's brother. She touches David's leg a lot and looks at him adoringly with her big brown eyes. I hate it so much, but there's no stopping it.

We do take an epic Christmas vacation though, to visit Anne and David's parents. Anne and her husband Rich, Jason and Alex, their black lab, Mary, my mom, and I all crowd into one vehicle and take the winding mountain roads eight hours north in a snowstorm, the flakes so furious we can't even roll down the windows when the dog farts.

When we get there, I am amazed by their grandma's cooking, even better than the Mennonites, and her beautiful table, set with a tablecloth and delicate Christmas china. We go sledding for so many hours my toes turn purple-blue and I sob as they thaw in tepid bathwater. We play the Monster Game with all the lights off and just the wood burning fire crackling. David hides somewhere down the hall and the four of us have to find him before he finds us and chases us back to safety, his sweatshirt over his head, his body crouched as he runs towards us. We squeal with terror and glee. He writes me a letter and tells me that he loves me, that he will be my dad and will take care of me. I can't put my finger on it, but his words make me uncomfortable.

There will be a wedding. I will have a new family, new grandparents, and friends-turned-cousins. We are going to pack up that old Chevy and drive north to a whole new part of the state.

The last time I walk into that public school, I am 12 years old and realize I will never have to smell the cafeteria again or see mean Julie. I'm leaving this town and my best grandma, and my horses, and the owl in the barn, but maybe I will never have to have the frozen feeling around men again. It's been bad lately but my memory bank is dark so I can't remember why. I just know it's time to blow this town.

Now seems like a good time to borrow a line from one of my favorite books, *The Hobbit*: "Escaping goblins to be caught by wolves!" In other words, "Out of the frying pan, into the fire." Here we go.

To the Outside Girl, with Love

Sweet little Jade, I am watching you, I am with you.

I have been here lifetime after lifetime and will never abandon you.

Your soul agreed to take this journey at this exact time, and I have given you the power of hope and optimism.

Even now, at your core, you recognize true empowerment comes through engaging with your life path, no matter how dark.

I love your free-spirited nature; no box can contain you.

You will grow, you will thrive, and someday you will become a woman who will know exactly how to keep yourself safe.

Imagine yourself as that woman now, walking into that tiny house and smiling.

Your smile is genuine, people know they can trust you.

First you hug your weary mama and tell her she's doing a good job, such a good job.

This love can cover anything and everything.

Fear, doubt, shame, and worry lose all their power in the face of this love.

You will translate that love to your mama in an instant and peace will fill her eyes, but she will also need a nap.

So you send her to rest and make dinner, and little Jade looks at you with adoration because you're so safe, so beautiful and powerful.

You are a protector, you are protected.

And when men like Jonathan come near the house, they take one look at your face and leave, knowing instantly that you would gladly kill them.

Your optimism, joy, and hope are not here to be taken advantage of, and will not be mistaken for ignorance.

The generational chains that entangle and trap your family are here for you to break. Make no mistake: what is happening is not fucking okay, my darling.

II

Teen Years

*"Having experienced her own disappearance, she is conscious of how important it is for people to be seen, so when she looks at them...she also looks **for** them, just in case they too have got lost and need finding." - Ann-Marie MacDonald*

3

Baby *Suddenly* Got Back

My class has been taking turns to read the stories we've written aloud in front of everyone. It's the second day of sharing, and I'm so excited and nervous it feels like 100 chickadees are flying around in my stomach when it's finally my turn. I've worked so hard on this story. It has a main character with violet eyes, who spends most of her time in the woods collecting amazing things and finding true love.

There are six other students in my 6th grade class, and the English teacher is our favorite, Mr. Callihan. He's tall with dark hair and a mustache and when he reads aloud, his voice puts me into a trance. I yearn to stay awake because Ray Bradburry's stories are the BEST, but my body gets so relaxed from the drone of his voice I almost fall asleep. I only hope I can meet his expectations and that everyone will be as impressed as I am with my own story.

I'm on the third page and things are going well, but the chickadees haven't settled, and there are so many feelings to deal with I just disappear out of myself and float to the top of the room to observe the hullabaloo so I don't get too overwhelmed. The problem is when I do that, no one is left in charge of my body. My voice keeps reading the words on the page but there's a hot trickle running down my legs and I can't do anything to stop it. I try to ignore it and keep reading but my eyes see there's a large wet spot on the carpet. I know I have to re-enter my body to deal with this mess and handle the shame.

I stop reading and motion to a girl named Laura at the front of the class. "Laura!" I hiss. The terror in my eyes translates and she looks at Mr. Callihan for permission. He nods, the rest of the class looking confused, as she stands up and walks over to me. "I've started my PERIOD like right now, and I need help. There's blood everywhere! Meet me in the bathroom."

I wrap my sweater around my waist and escape to the safety of the bathroom stall. In the school office, they call my new almost-grandma to help because my mom works the night shift and sleeps while we're at school. Mary and my mom and I live in a basement apartment, and David lives with his parents because my mom and David are not married yet, just engaged and planning the wedding, and no one wants anyone living in sin.

My almost-grandma, who is just as kind and loving as her daughter Anne, brings me big, thick pads to put in my underwear, and clean clothes, including socks, which is brilliant of her. I hadn't considered my wet socks, still not fully back in my body.

Laura comes to check in with me later in the day and tells me that she helped clean up the mess on the carpet.

"That definitely wasn't blood, just so you know," she says, slowly.

Oh, I do know. There's definitely no need for the gigantic diaper pad hanging out in my underwear either, but when you're 13, starting your period in front of the class is a much better story than peeing your pants like a baby. When in doubt, control the narrative.

As it turns out, there's a pretty steep price to pay for leaving your body and watching everything happen so you don't have to deal with your feelings. I don't have a lot of bad memories of the frozen times living in my head, but I've peed my pants quite a few times and I have an insatiable need to touch myself to bring myself comfort, to scratch what itches. This, apparently, is a sin so I try and keep it under wraps, but it's a pretty constant, pressing need. I also crave attention from boys. I just love the boys. If I can get their attention, it makes me feel seen. I like the shy boys best. The loud ones are too easy.

The wedding happens; it can't be stopped. The nice thing about the wedding is the pretty, peach satin dress with a big bow that my new grandma sews for me, a bigger one for me, and a smaller, matching dress for Mary so we can be bridesmaids. We go back to the bottom of Idaho to the Baptist church for the wedding, and Jan Kimberley makes the wedding cake out of carob. It's disgusting.

There are big changes all around when David enters the picture on a daily basis. My mom is besotted, but they fight a lot. David rules with an iron fist because he's the leader of the home, the head of the house, the head honcho. He requests that white things and chocolate return to the table, so I finally get biscuits and proper cake again. He demands we call him Dad. When I complain about how I have to explain my name to everyone, he suggests I take on a new spelling along with his last name. He hasn't officially adopted us, but we are no longer "Abshire". We are now "Kohl" and overnight my name changes from Jade Abshire to J-a-d-e-y Kohl. He demands we are polite and respectful, but I don't know what he means by that half the time. I have very few moments of happiness during this transition, just a lot of darkness and confusion.

One day we're at a park playing frisbee and my new grandma Mertie and grandpa Fred are there. They really are great, but I don't call them Grandpa and Grandma. I've already had those before in my life.

The grandpa is looking around for someone to pass the Frisbee to, and I squeal, "Over here Freddie!!" I hold out my hands and the sun is on my face, and in that brief moment, I'm an outside girl again, free and happy.

Suddenly the shadow of David is big and scary and right beside me. I look up as he grabs my arm.

"You will NEVER disrespect people like that again," he snaps. "My father is an adult and you will call him Mr. Kohl or Grandpa."

The scared feeling in the pit of my stomach is mostly confusion. I have no idea what this dude is so ramped up about. This sudden boiling over is constant and I never know what will bring it on. We are meant to never talk about the time B.D. (Before David). This is our life now. We are a family, we are proper.

One afternoon I take *The Scarlet Letter* off the shelf to read and realize

Hester Prynne and my mom have something in common: my mom wears a big fat A of shame on her chest. Mary and I are the living proof. If I ask about my dad, which I do all the time, I am met with a potent combination of anger and shame. I only know that his name is also David. I ask about Mary's dad once, and decide to never make that mistake again. Every time I walk alone, I imagine my real dad is trying to find me. A few times cars driven by men slow down as they pass by me, and I get a thrill from thinking, hoping, that it just might be him.

The next few years are a blur on the family front. There's no safe place for me as my body changes. My legs are too hairy and I finally need a tampon and plus sized pads. I know I can't ask for help and spend a few painful months with the cardboard piece of the tampon stuck inside until I realize it's the "applicator" referred to on the box. My mom is terrified of all these changes and can't help me; she is no longer my anchor. I can see it makes her sad when David yells at me, but she wants me to be a proper, good girl-woman and she thinks this is best. Mary is too young and we are shoved into tiny bedrooms together with zero privacy so there's nowhere for me to go. I can tell Mary wants me to be her protector, but most of the time I'm just mean. Our tiny apartment can't have dogs, so Fresh lives with Mertie and Fred and when I see her I just feel empty inside, even when she wants to play.

My mom has another baby. His name is Brian. This wakes me up a little, I have to admit. He is the sweetest and cutest boy ever born. He has my mom's huge brown eyes and I love him so much.

Our tiny, two bedroom basement apartment is moldy and too small now, so we move into the trailer park. It's depressing with its dark paneled walls and postage stamp spaces, but somehow our backyard faces an actual forest so there's always places to go and trees to climb. David is a class A gardener, just like his dad. He plants roses, a huge garden builds up in the backyard, and he trims the birch tree in the front. He spends a lot of time splitting wood for the small wood stove that heats the whole trailer so well we have to open the windows in the winter. It's dark and grimy in the trailer so David painstakingly paints the fake wood paneling white and just like that we have covered the past and have a fresh start.

A year and a half later, my mom has another baby, named Kallie. She's an adorable screamer, with bright blue eyes and curly blonde hair. I feel trapped in the trailer, so mostly I just read. My punishment for bad behavior is to have my books taken from me. My mom is very picky about what I can and cannot read, so I'm mostly stuck with David's bookshelf and books. I read all day: *A Connecticut Yankee in King Arthur's Court, Watership Down, Jane Eyre, Wuthering Heights, Great Gatsby,* and even *A Tale of Two Cities.* We go to the library every week and my mom looks at my books and decides if they're too trashy. We don't have a TV, but that's nothing new for us, and we only listen to Christian music or classical music on the stereo in the living room.

There is a man behind the curtain in all of this, a main character in my story. His name is Doug Wilson. Now, D-O-U-G is not GOD spelled backwards, right? But no one in our new church seems to know this. At first glance, he's a jolly bearded man who plays the guitar and sings with joy. He has kindness in his eyes and seems fair and steady. The school I go to, Logos School, is a new school he started, and the church attached is his too. He is a Bible-believing Christian, which apparently means a lot of things I didn't know, but I'm about to learn.

It starts with the foundation, "families as God intended." This means one man, one woman, and arrows in your quiver. The man is the head of the house, the priest of his home. His word is law for his family. As long as his family is in order, meaning his wife is modest, submissive, making babies, and raising them, and his children are eager to learn and obedient, that is proof he is living God's plan and can be left alone. You can have lots of money and a big TV and nice cars, you can watch modern movies, or you can be piss poor and militant (that's us). It doesn't matter as long as you're all playing your roles. If you want to know what those roles are, don't worry, Doug knows and he will tell you. He says a man is a hammer, a woman a teacup. You wouldn't want a hammer in the kitchen or at a tea party, and you certainly wouldn't want to bring a teacup to go hunting, build a house, or protect the family.

Basically, women belong in the home, men belong everywhere else, and their collective job is to raise their family in such a shiny and attractive way that we will slowly but surely claim the entire culture for Christ.

Doug is the priest of the church, but we just call him pastor. If you have any questions, the fathers go and ask him directly and the women can ask his wife, Nancy. They have answers for everything and write books about it, so you can read their books along with the Bible.

When we first get to his church, Doug baptizes us in water as we commit our lives to Christ. But he changes his mind and says the Bible teaches you to baptize your babies when they're born, so God knows you mean to raise them properly and they will be saved. Not everyone gets to be saved, though, even if they want to. Only the chosen. You have to be picked. But not to worry! If you want to be chosen, it probably means you are.

There are more rules to follow than I can keep up with. In order to be a proper priest of your home, and keep everyone in order, you need to send your children to his Bible-based school. You can homeschool if you can't afford his school, he will even provide the curriculum if you pay for it, but it is a sin to use the public school system because it's impossible to raise your children in the way of the Lord in a heathen environment. Besides, public schools are trash, with a below-standard curriculum.

Doug has discovered a more godly form of education, what he calls a classical education. Christians have become a laughing stock in the current culture, he says, it's time to bring them back to relevance, and that starts with excellence and indoctrination.

We learn Latin, rhetoric, logic, we debate, we are encouraged to read all the classics in literature. This is not hard for me in the slightest. We have a whole semester on the Civil War and different teachers debate the North versus the South as if they are the generals of the war themselves. I'm on a long walk one day when I get a clear picture of which side Doug is on. I see him and Nancy raising a giant Confederate flag on our school's flagpole, proudly taking pictures of it waving in the wind.

It's beyond confusing to suddenly have every human with a penis either looking right at you or sending you electric currents of frantic energy. There are definitely some girls that give me the same feeling. But ultimately, I'm attracted to shy humans because I like to get in deep and have a conversation, get to know them, see what makes them tick, and let them know that I really see them. The look in their eyes when I've found the real them fills me up, but this ability, coupled with my new boobs and who-knows-what-else (I think it's my bottom?) apparently makes me dangerous. Attractive, intelligent women are admired in Doug's empire. Childbearing hips and a smart mind will build God's army. Too much spice, however, is treated like a ticking time bomb.

The almost all male teachers tell us that many women, in fact most women, are ready for marriage, and need to be married very early to have an outlet for their sexiness, to start bearing children for the Lord, and to have their mate's protection from other men's lustful gazes. I get the feeling that if they had their druthers, they would marry us off directly after starting our periods, like the biblical days or the days of the Roman Empire. My Bible and math teacher, Mr. Nance, tells our 7th grade class how glorious it would be to return to the Many Wives Law of the Old Testament days, but alas, he must obey the New Testament law of only one wife. You see, the male teachers are also the priests of their homes, almost all of them also go to the church, and they are a bit drunk on their power.

I pick up one of Doug's magazines in our trailer and read an article called, "Wine, Women, and Psalms," which tells all the men to drink, have a lot of sex, and sing as they build God's Kingdom. Drink wine (not to excess), you can only have sex with your wives (but don't worry, the Bible says they have to give it to you whenever you want it), and sing the Psalms set to music (in five-part harmony).

My adolescent brain is haphazardly piecing all of this information together and I feel like I'm repeating the social patterns of my youth: I am too shiny, I am always in trouble, I am constantly side-eyed by the girls, but most of the time I dissociate. I stay floating above my body which allows me to not care too much.

In 8th grade I'm given a hand-me-down sweater. It is emerald green and a bit too big, but I love the way it slips off on one side. I spend time in the mirror admiring the line of my neck and the curve of my shoulder before I go to school. The whole day, I'm acutely aware of the coolness I feel on my skin when it slides down. It's a great feeling; it reminds me of the sun on my face, of the freedom of being an outside girl. But at the end of English class, Mr. Sample asks me to stay behind and tells the other girls to shut the door behind them so we can have privacy.

"Do you know what a harlot is?" he asks me. I don't. "Do you know what 'whore' means?" Nope, I don't know that either. He's asking me in a gentle, quiet voice, with the smallest of smirks playing at the corner of his mouth, but it sure doesn't feel safe to me. The rest of his words are garbled by my brain, something about how Proverbs tell of women who lead men to slaughter and destruction with the power of seduction.

He ends with one final question, a small smile still playing on his lips.

"Do you want to go to hell?"

I respond by matching his smile, making my lips land in a position which, I hope, hides my incredulous terror at being talked to so baldly by a man, a teacher no less. I mumble something about being late to class and leave in a daze. My classmates look at me, ask me what happened, but I push my feelings, which are a confusing combination of embarrassment and shame, down, down, deep down, and say nothing to anyone, ever.

Some teachers really do care and bring light wherever they are. You don't have to have a teaching degree to teach at Logos, you just need to be a godly example and know some things about the subject matter. Bonus points if you're passionate about it.

Mrs. Davis is our young, lively science teacher. She's just finished college and her honeymoon. She takes us on a field trip to the anatomy lab at WSU and shocks us with a naked dead man cadaver in the middle of the room. His penis has long, gray hairs sprouting from it, and his head is sawed in half so we can view his brain.

"It's a hemisection of his brain!" Mrs Davis explains, breathlessly. She's a little flustered herself and tries her hardest to keep the field trip educational. We are all a middle school mess though, giggling uncontrollably or almost fainting. One unfortunate boy throws up.

There's a jar with a strange blob. We can see a tooth and some hairs coming out of it. Mrs. Davis explains that it came from the uterus of a 19 year old girl who was told she was pregnant but cried out for justice, insisting she was pure, a virgin. It turned out the baby was just this very cyst, now in a jar. She nods with holy wisdom while she tells a group of girls this story. I don't even really understand how women get pregnant, because my mom can't speak of such things, it's not taught at school, and I don't have a TV, but I have an idea because the books I read on my own deal with themes like this all the time. *Anna Karenina*? Please. I'm enthralled.

The principal of the school, Mr. Garfield, loves theater and starts a drama department. The stage fits me like my perfectly worn-in skates. I feel alive, seen, and comfortable taking a script, becoming the character, and making everyone else believe I am too. I get most of the main roles and am one of the principal's favorites, which gives me a serious layer of protection from my bad girl reputation.

Just like the Mennonite days, the weird Christian school days, and the public school days, I can't seem to summon the reverence and respect I yearn for. Even though I am trying my hardest, I am still not believable as a good Christian girl. There's a storm of injustice brewing in my 14 year old core; it's time for my strong skater legs to start kicking again.

4

It's Goin' Down for Reals

I don't get out much, but miraculously my mom and stepdad have let me go to a football game with a group of girls. Not just any game, a college football game at the Kibbie Dome. I love it there; it manages to be both cozy and bright, and is full of noises, people, and exciting things.

My core is humming and I feel alive all the way to the tips of my fingers. Every time I turn around there's a boy, much older than me, staring right at me, not caring that I keep catching him looking. He's the center of his group. Everyone with him is touching his arm, punching his shoulder, trying to get his attention, but he is laser-focused on me and me alone. I like it, but I don't do anything more than flash a smile in his direction once in a while to let him know I don't mind his attention. A girl in my group recognizes him from when she went to public school for one year. She says he's the quarterback, the most popular boy at the high school, a senior! This makes me laugh out loud. Why would he be looking at me?

Later that night, the phone rings. It's for me, a boy. I don't get calls from boys so I'm confused. My mom gives me a strange look when she hands me the phone, and I stretch the brown cord as far as it will go down the hall before I say hello. It's him. It's Scott the Quarterback. He's found my number, he admits with a laugh. He says it was hard to do. I know, with a mix of excitement and dread, that I will do very dangerous things to be with this boy, and it starts with the lie I tell when I hang up the phone.

"That was Josh," I say to my mother. "He was reminding me about our project due on Monday."

This feels like an opportunity, an honor. I have been chosen.

Being with Scott is overstimulating. The effort it takes to pretend like I know how to be with him is exhausting, not to mention the series of intricate lies I have to keep up with. I sneak out during lunch and meet him at the McDonald's across the street. He loves my emerald sweater; he says my shoulder is sexy. I start going to the Nazarene church's youth group so Scott can intercept me in his truck and take me out. When I get in, he complains that I don't wear perfume and makes fun of my KMart shoes. We go to R rated movies, another first for me, and they are so fascinating and horrible I can't help but get wrapped up in the story, even while Scott's hands grope at me. I have him over while I'm babysitting. One night he's there, on top of me and keeps sucking and kissing my neck. To be fair, I do ask him to, but he's not very good at it. He wants to do more and keeps trying to take my jeans off, but I manage to push him off and send him home.

The next day is Sunday, and I have a hickey on my neck. We're smack dab in the middle of summer, so wearing my one and only turtleneck sweater to church will look more than a little fishy. I weigh my options as I curl my hair. There aren't many. I take a deep breath and hold the curling iron on the hickey as long as I can stand the sizzling pain. I scream as part of the act and my mother comes running in. I cry and tell her I've burned myself, but the irony is that I've done so in more ways than one. The jig is up. A girl at the youth group rats me out, the six year old I was babysitting tells her parents she saw a boy on top of me in the living room, and I run out of ways to get to the McDonald's during lunch time. I am in all the trouble. The consequences are swift and fierce and I am full of shame. I've watched R rated movies and had a boy kiss my neck and rub up on me. But the web of lies I've told is what makes me feel like the proverbial whore Mr. Sample foretold the year before.

My stepfather is clearly not in control of his family (i.e. me) which means he is failing as the priest of his home. He's the 5th grade teacher at the school, which covers Mary's and my tuition and the entire staff is invested in keeping me pure. My stepfather makes photocopies of the behavior section of the report card and every Friday I have to take a sheet around to all of my teachers to have them answer five questions about my performance that week. Each question is answered with 1) Poor 2) Fair 3) Good. If I get one "Poor" mark, I'm grounded for the week. "Talking During Class" gets me pretty much every time. Mr. Callihan, still my favorite, chuckles softly under his mustache when he gives me Poor marks. I laugh with him, and beg him to change it to Fair, and if I stay and banter with him, sometimes he will, but mostly I'm grounded all week, every week. One Saturday the whole family is loaded in the car to go to a wedding. When we get there, my stepfather turns to me and tells me, since I am grounded, I will be staying in the car while the rest of the family attends.

All of this does very little to make me holy. I am more disrespectful than ever. I am sulky, I don't do my chores properly, I forget things, and lose things left and right. I'm so bad about losing things that I could lose my coat in a blizzard. That's not a turn of phrase; I literally do just that. More public school boys find me, college boys find me, and sometimes I have them over while I'm babysitting, but I'm sure to never get a hickey again, so mostly we sit and awkwardly stare at each other. I don't know what to do with the boys, I just want their attention. I'm not willing to go further than flirting and an occasional kiss, but there's also a buzzing need, just below my stomach, and I long for someone who knows what to do with it.

I am the bane of my stepfather's existence. I feel trapped. The minute I turn 16 I find a help wanted ad in the newspaper and ride my bike to the Pizza Hut. I know I want to work here, to be a waitress and make tips, so I walk right in and tell that to the manager. He smirks and asks me how much experience I have. None, I say. But I flirt with him like I'm begging for a Fair or Good mark at the end of a school week and I get the job. My stepfather is convinced I'll be fired in a week as it's clear to him that I don't know the meaning of work and respect.

I get myself to work on my bike. It gets stolen off our back porch one day because I forgot to put the lock on, so I walk the five miles round trip to work and back. No one feels sorry for me. I'm reminded that my stepfather rides his bike every day, in every kind of weather, to work or to run errands so my mom can have our one car. He even rides to church most Sundays so he won't be late. He abhors being late, and doesn't trust my mom to get all the smaller kids ready, me out of bed, and everyone in the car to get him to the church on time.

I work as many hours as they'll give me, double shifts even, and save most of my tips, carefully tithing 10%. This gets me out of the trailer as much as possible. Now I have plenty to buy a new bike, I can buy my own clothes, shoes, and perfume, and anytime there's a ski trip or a whitewater rafting trip I pay my way and pay for my gear. These outside trips are constant and easily the best part of school. I learn how to downhill ski and nearly every time I choose a trail that's tricky, but without too many moguls, so I can go as fast as possible, straight down the hill. It's one of the only places I feel completely in my body, but not weighed down by its realness, especially when we ski at night. In the dark everything is whisper-quiet and lost in the shadows. When I look up I can see flakes of snow dancing in the lights, but the light can't reach the vastness of the mountain and I feel rooted, grounded, free.

It's now June and the Parker family is having an end of the year party. The Parker girls are famous at our school: three beautiful and confident girls with plenty of money. Their father, Charlie, is a lawyer. Charlie has control of his home, and everyone looks up to him. There will be a live band and folk dancing. I beg to go but my stepfather says no, even though I'm not grounded that week. It's a no simply because there will be dancing and I'm not allowed to dance. I beg some more and finally sign a contract that states I will go to the party, but only to socialize, and will not participate in the dancing.

The Parker house is big and bright and lively. The living and dining room have been cleared, and the door is open to showcase the band outside on the porch. The thrumming feeling activates in my fingers, in my belly. The oldest Parker girl, Madison, is dancing with a boy who's not from our school, so close that it can only mean they'll be engaged soon. I'm in awe of her. I sit along the wall to watch everyone. I've never danced before, not in a group anyway, not WITH someone, and my eyes are shining with the thought of how it would feel to move that way, with joy and abandon.

Charlie, still handsome in a father/old man way, comes up to me and holds out his hands.

"You came to my party and you're not dancing!? This is a party for dancing, come!"

I hang my head and mumble something about not knowing how to dance, which is a lie. My body knows how to dance. Apparently Charlie knows a lie when he hears one, so he grabs my hands and swirls me to the middle of the floor.

The next two hours are a blur; I never stop dancing. I find partners who know what they're doing and keep up with the twists and twirls. It's skating but better. The outside girl in me is alive and kicking.

Almost as an act of rebellion, I come clean about the dancing the very next morning, arguing that it would have been rude not to honor the host's request, explaining the innocence of it all. There's zero quarter given as I have dishonored my contract. I am grounded for two weeks and given extra chores.

The funny thing is that soon after my shameful transgression, Doug decides everyone should learn to dance, but because they call it traditional or folk dancing, and call it "balls," it's acceptable. The school begins to teach students young and old how to dance. They introduce ballroom dancing because there is athleticism and chivalry in the art of a boy offering his hand, a girl accepting, the boy escorting her on the dance floor with authority, and leading with strength in the dance while she follows. The strongest leader and the most graceful follower make the best couple and look good to everyone else. This is a perfect analogy for a proper marriage. So now I'm allowed to dance, but the shine is long gone.

By the time I get to 10th grade I am truly exhausted. I can't keep actively playing the rebel - it's too much work - so I decide to finally put in some effort. I get up early to read my Bible, I underline passages, I make myself feel something in the words. I stop being okay with failing math, and go to Mr. Nance's house almost every day for help with my homework. I get As on homework, Bs on quizzes, and Ds or Fs on tests, which averages out to a C. My stepfather is fine with this.

"C means average," he says. "Not everyone 'excels' at everything. It's okay to have a few Cs." Is this comforting? I think so.

One of my friends, Lila, and I join a choir at a church in a neighboring town. You have to try out to be in this choir, and in the summer we get uniforms and travel around the west coast, singing at malls and churches, and helping with VBS (Vacation Bible School) camps. I love it, and not just because the choir teacher's son, Cody, is into me. He's funny - the life of the party. I've been given permission to date Christian boys interviewed by David now that I'm 16, so I tell him if he wants to date me he has to ask my father's permission.

An interview is set in my stepfather's classroom and Cody is escorted to a 5th grader's desk. David sits at his desk and grills him with questions. I wait outside the door. Cody is sweating when he comes out and he looks terrified, but he passed. So now we go on dates, mostly PG movies where we grope each other without getting anywhere. It's like NO ONE knows how to scratch what itches. But I remind myself to behave as a Christian.

Cody plays the trumpet in a band. He's actually very talented so it's fun to watch him play. I go to his concerts as often as I can and my heart swells with pride.

I meet his dad and their best family friend, someone special they are deeply fond of: Sgt. Mark of the Pullman police department, if you please. When he meets me, he grabs my hand with his meaty fingers and holds it for a long time, laughing at some unknown joke when he finally lets go.

One night, Cody is taking me to dinner. He's picked me up in Moscow and we're driving to Pullman where he lives to eat at a Chinese place he likes. Suddenly sirens blare. A cop car has materialized behind us and we're being pulled over. Cody looks like he's about to faint and I tell him we aren't speeding, nothing is wrong, it will be okay.

"I know it's him. I know it's him!" he moans, and hits the steering wheel with his fist as he pulls to the side of the road.

It is "HIM" I guess, Sgt. Mark of the meaty fingers. He saunters up, hat pulled down, and slaps the hood of the car like a cowboy riding its mare. Then he braces his arms against either side of the window jam.

"Are you two behavin'?" he drawls.

Cody's laugh is loud and his voice cracks. I'm baffled and look from Cody to Sgt. Mark, trying to figure out the dynamic. After a strange conversation which may as well have been in a familial secret code, Sgt. Mark smacks the car one more time and stares at Cody before walking back to his car. We continue on as if nothing happened.

Our choir goes on tour and Lila and I get to be roommates. We put sunless tanning lotion on our legs and wash our hands right after so there's no streaks on our palms. One of our uniforms sports white shorts, and we roll the bottoms up to make them shorter. The tour is actually a lot of hard work: two concerts a day and work in between. We're spreading God's love. It takes commitment.

On a rare day off, Cody and I are walking on the beach at the Oregon coast. I love it here and feel the stillness and peace in my bones. I can stay in my body here. I see a rock, bigger than the rest in its pile and shaped in an interesting, imperfect oval with a stripe running across it.

"This is you," I say, handing him the rock. He looks at me, questioning. "See, you stand out from the rest. You're noticeable. But you're not perfect. That bothers you, I know. You're too hard on yourself, Cody. You don't need to be perfect. Your 'different' is not 'weird.' It's okay to be yourself." I'm surprised but thrilled to see tears spring to his eyes.

"H-h-h-ow do you know that!" he stutters, now fully crying.

I'm a bit dismayed at how effective my words have been and pat his back, rubbing his shoulder. We keep talking as we wander down the beach, and I know there's something more that he's not telling me.

It's not long after this interaction that I realize I'm done and bored with Cody. He's become a puppy dog, following me with his big blue eyes and panting every time I'm around. I want a man. Actually, I have no idea what I want, but something in me feels like Cody's broken and my own brokenness can't handle it, so I break up with him. He cries again and asks if he can still call and talk to me, insisting I'm one of his best friends. I say yes, he can, and he does. He calls me often.

One day I'm alone in the trailer, a rarity, so I am more focused during our call than usual. When I feel calm like this, I can be fully in my body with no part of me floating away. We're not even talking about Sgt. Mark, but I'm suddenly struck with a lightning bolt of awareness and the words come before I can stop them.

"Cody, Sgt. Mark is hurting you and it has to stop."

The effect on Cody is electric. He stutters and stammers and denies, but I just keep repeating, keeping my voice low and even, "Sgt. Mark is hurting you and it has to stop."

Cody tells me with fractured words what's been happening and I piece the rest together well enough. Sgt. Mark takes him "fishing" on his boat, and that's where "it" happens. Mark is his best friend, Cody says, they tell each other everything, but there's just this one thing that happens and every time Mark promises it won't happen again. He cries and makes promises and Cody knows he's trying so hard to not do it. Cody is saving him, teaching him how to stop.

I need to hang up, I'm getting overwhelmed so I try to change the subject, lamely asking what he's doing for the weekend.

"I'm leaving in a few hours for two days on the boat with Mark," he tells me.

My response is a barely coherent cry-yell-scream. I tell him he can't go with that man again and to hang on, I'm finding him some help.

I hang up and my mind casts a net, desperately trying to catch something. I can drive but I don't have a car; I'll need a ride. But I can't handle Sgt. Mark by myself. My parents are gone, but even if they were here I don't trust them to understand, to deal with it properly. I think of Mr. Wilson. Not Doug, but his father, Jim. Jim is the pastor of another church and I've been sent to him before for counseling. Our congregation goes to pastors, and occasionally their wives, for "counseling"; we don't use therapists. Jim is nice, and he knows things. He can see into my soul and still smiles at me with his mouth and all the way up to his eyes. I've only met with him a few times, but he is the only person I trust enough to call.

He asks me a few clarifying questions before he says, "I'll pick you up in ten minutes. Please call Cody back and tell him to not leave with the sergeant. Tell him help is coming." I leave a note for my parents that says I've gone to see Jim Wilson, not a lie, but not the whole truth either.

Mr. Wilson and I drive the 20 minutes to Cody's house in Pullman. We say words to each other, but I don't really hear him, or know what my responses are. The problem is that I don't understand exactly how Cody is being hurt, but my body somehow knows it's how I've been hurt before. I have no memories of anything, or even know how I was hurt, but my body remembers; it's just not something I'm able or willing to put into words.

I now understand sex, the penis-in-vagina kind, and I know the Bible talks about how men lying with men as with a woman is an abomination, and women sleeping together is contrary to nature. But how can men be with men? There are no vaginas present for that. I imagine women together, rubbing their vaginas, their boobs, lots of fingers and tongues involved, and that makes sense to me, even making the area below my tummy tighten in a pleasant way. Men have no vaginas, so they can only touch and lick each other's penises. But the bible says lying with men AS WITH a woman. I can't wrap my mind around it.

I keep trying to put the pieces of the puzzle together as we drive and drive for what feels like forever. And then it hits me. Men don't have a vagina, but they do have another hole. Sgt. Mark is LITERALLY putting his penis in Cody's butthole without his permission. I try to keep my jaw from hanging open. My face turns bright red and I am more frantic than ever to get to Cody's house and put a stop to this. I also file away the fact that buttholes can be involved in sex in general. Fascinating. I'll need more time to consider that concept later.

Once we get there we knock briskly on the door. Cody is so anxious he's shaking, he won't even look at me, he even seems angry. Cody's parents appear somewhere between confused and surprised. Jim introduces himself formally and asks to speak to them and Cody privately, which means I can't listen. Dang. I wanted to be part of this. I wanted to hold Cody's hand and give him the courage to speak. I know he needs it.

They come back out to the living room where I've been impatiently waiting for about 20 minutes. Cody's mom is crying.

"I just don't know about all of this. This can't be happening. He's our closest family friend, a respected member of this community, a deacon in our church. He's on the police force for goodness sake!" she rambles through her tears.

Cody looks like he wants to crawl into the walls. I don't understand why his mom isn't hugging him and screaming about how she wants to kill Sgt. Mark. We leave. I feel let down.

I don't have to feel let down for long before Sgt. Mark gets arrested. A whole bunch of other boys come forward and say he was doing the same thing to them. It starts with a 21 year old who says it happened to him just the same way, from ages 14 to 18. In a counseling session, Jim tells me I did a good job, but other than that one time I don't talk about it with anyone. Ever. I just push it down, down, down, and say nothing.

A few months later, Lila and I get invited to be camp counselors at the summer camp connected to Cody's church. Lila is dating Cody's best friend Adam, so the four of us work with the little kids during the day and have time to talk, swim, and hike in the evenings.

Cody and I feel awkward around each other. I feel weird in general. Cody is clearly not okay. Part of me wants to look at the adults and ask them how the heck they are letting us be in charge of little kids after we've just been through this horrible thing that hasn't even been put into words? But instead I put on lots of mascara and laugh a lot while I help the kids with their craft projects and make sure they get to their next activity while doing the teenage-typical bare minimum of work.

One night Adam turns to me and grabs my hands. I hear him say Sgt. Mark was hurting him too. He says he wanted to kill himself because he didn't know how to stop it.

"You saved my life by stopping this. Thank you," he says, with tears in his eyes. He's the only one who has ever thanked me, but I'm not looking for that. I mostly feel confused by the whole thing, tired and empty, and certainly not ready to be anyone's savior.

This Christian girl thing is so hard. I want to be good but I hate feeling like I'm stuck in a box. I let myself float away most of the time, disconnecting from my body, and observing myself do horrible things.

There are six people in my class total: three boys and three girls. Jon, John, Josh, Kari, Sarah, and me. I cannot relate to any of them. Kari and Sarah are kind. Jon and John are so incredibly smart. But I am mean to them all. I ignore them, tease them cruelly, and flirt with Josh to make his face turn red.

Josh is a cutie. With bright blue eyes and dark hair, I want to love him and he wants to love me, but I feel too empty to love and he's too shy. So I just touch his arm, lean into him, and feel his longing.

When I do hang out with anyone, it's with the girls from the grade below me: Lila, Heather, and a few others. I am loud with them. I laugh and talk really fast, I go shopping and buy jeans and big white button up shirts from the Gap, and I put extra makeup on between classes. The holy girls watch me with horror and dismay. I feel lonely the whole time. There's a huge hole where my heart should be, so I try to fill it with extras of everything.

To the Outside Girl, with Love

The wind in your hair has always whispered to you, reminding you that you are seen, you are held.

All this time you thought you were simply experiencing the wind, but it turns out she loves to kiss you back.

A gentle teacher.

Listen!

She tells you fear is simply courage becoming known, and tears are unspoken words finding their voice.

Dearest one, you will always be a girl saved by Gaia.

Your feet find your way to her.

You seek her in the sun, the cold, the rain.

You don't realize how many times I've compelled you up the hill, just outside the prison of your house where there is no place for you to be still in your mind.

You can always be present with Mother Earth.

When you imagine a safe place, it's in the woods by the water.

That place? It's real. I'm taking you there.

Be patient my love, there are many roads to travel, but the Sun, the Wind, the Rain, and blankets of Snow will be your companions.

Follow along my darling.

You are not alone.

III

The Reaping

"I told you I wanted to live in a world in which the antidote to shame is not honor, but honesty." Maggie Nelson

5

How to Fake It 'Til You Make It

Ella San is a registered Sorrel Quarter Horse, the best girl ever. Ella is so fast and skilled that my Aunt Mona once won the state championship for barrel racing on her back, but she is my mother's pride and joy through and through.

My mother rides Ella bareback on the dunes all day and neither of them ever gets tired. They love one another deeply. My mom is her best, whole self when she is on or around a horse, especially Ella. My mom was still in high school when I was born and she couldn't keep ownership of Ella when we finally moved into town, so she made a deal with my grandpa: Ella would belong to my grandpa and Ella's first colt would belong to me. And so it was done.

When I was around 10 years old, Ella finally popped out a strong chestnut colt that I got to call my own. My grandpa said I had to name it after him, which I believed until my mother told me otherwise. But I wanted to please him and I loved the name Jim Buck, so here we are.

Jim Buck is tall for an American Quarter Horse, 16 hands, and so gentle and beautiful. But we moved up north just a few years after he was born and now, years later, I am a raging ball of hormones trying to make my way in the world. I need a car. So I have my grandpa sell Jim Buck, send me the money, and I find an old Grand Am in great condition. The only problem is that it's a stick shift and learning how to drive her is excruciating. I've never really gotten the hang of steep hills and am convinced I'm going to roll back and crash into someone.

Since the Fuehrers are now family, not just friends, we continue to see them over the years even though they still live in southern Idaho. Jason, just a year younger than me, is now my cousin-not-cousin-by-blood so it frees us up to hang out and be more comfortable around each other. As we get older, there is a confusing, unspoken attraction, but we just turn it into genuine interest in getting to know everything about one another. We go so far as to write each other letters between get-togethers. It's clear even in the moment that we're growing up together. He is one of my very best friends and I feel safe with him. We all feel safe together in my grandparents' house. They never make me feel like less than blood, even though I came into the picture an already ornery teenager.

My grandma teaches me to sew and makes me clothes anytime I express interest in wearing them. She is the best cook I've ever known. My grandpa is the only human in the world who can whistle and not make me want to crawl out of my skin. He trills like a songbird, but it's never shrill. Their house is the epitome of safety and peace.

It's been a year since the Sgt. Mark debacle and I feel like I am coming together nicely. I feel some sense of control. This Christian girl thing isn't so bad after all. I just had to know where to give in and follow the rules: smile, but not too much, laugh, just not too loud, and most of all, don't attract attention. That one I'm still not great at, even when I try really hard.

My body has not gotten the memo, however. It's to the point where I hate going places with my mom because she chides me for the way I walk. I remember her face of horror when I emerged from the local swimming pool in my pale pink suit a while back. It had taken us HOURS to find a one-piece that fit my long torso and wouldn't crawl up my butt. This ugly pink contraption was lined, but apparently still see through when wet, something we couldn't have known until its first use. From then on, the message remains consistent: I am dangerous, even when I try to be good.

One day, I get to attend the Youth Government at the state capitol in Boise. We meet other schools there, even public schools, and pretend to be state senators and representatives and hold sessions. It's mostly boring, but I bought myself a white power suit and put my curled hair up with a pearl-studded banana clip, so I look and feel amazing.

All day, I see boys looking at me with admiration, and girls not liking it quite as much. I'm so distracted by this dynamic that in the middle of a session in the senate chamber, I suddenly realize I can't wait for the bathroom a moment longer. When I sit down on the toilet, a huge ball of blood the size of a lime plops into the toilet. Blood gushes everywhere, and is already covering the back of my beautiful new suit. Clearly, that had been the cause of the unexpected pressure I had mistaken for needing to pee, and now I've got a problem.

It takes me two hours to spy someone from my group from the top of the rotunda, where I stand as still as possible scoping out my options. I finally get the attention of Jeana, who now has to find our teacher, get the keys to the van, and bring me my bags so I can change. Needless to say, she is more than a little annoyed with me.

When I finally emerge from the bathroom in a fresh, less flashy outfit, toting my ruined suit in the plastic garbage bag from the bathroom, I pretend not to be embarrassed, but the news of my bloody exit has spread. Everyone is whispering behind their hands and laughing at me. I get clots all the time and bleed randomly (so much blood), but it isn't something I talk about. I don't share that with anyone. I push it all down, way down, and say nothing. Besides, I can count the number of times I've been to the doctor on one hand. We don't have health insurance. My mom is trained as a nurse and can assess cuts, bruises, and burns, and the rest of the body, mind, and soul we leave to God. It's a good thing I have straight teeth.

For one year only, Ben, the most amazing boy, comes to Logos. He is two years younger than me, but we are drawn to each other like magnets. Like me, he is a little different from everyone else, shy but wicked smart and sarcastic. He knows how to stay under the radar, to not get in trouble, and I watch and learn from him as much as I can. We spend all our lunches together, as well as any breaks we have.

Over Christmas break, he goes to Hawaii and still finds time to call me. He brings me back the most delicate anklet, a silver blue dolphin dangling from a thin gold chain. A few weeks later, the entire high school is watching a movie in the auditorium and some of us elect to sit on the floor. Ben half-leans on my lap and I play with his hair a bit as he mindlessly strokes my arm. I feel so safe here with him. We share a nurturing type of love with the promise of something more.

The next day my stepfather calls me into his classroom and berates me for openly flirting, for shaming myself with another boy. I am confused. He hadn't been there and it had been dark. Who was watching us? Regardless, I am grounded for a week.

I wander back to class, ashamed but also angry. I start to relay the unfairness of my story to Sarah, but Mr. Callihan interrupts.

"Jade. I'm the one who spoke to your father about your behavior with Ben. You can't get that close to a boy. There are consequences. Overt flirting like that isn't tolerated. You know the rules." He softens his words to make us laugh over something trivial, and lets me know he only had my best interest at heart. He tells me I need to understand my power over men and use it wisely. I feel less stupid by the end of his explanation.

A few people from my school are chosen for another Youth Government project and this time we get to stay overnight in the dorms at BSU. I put on my trusty white shorts, roll them up, and a few of the girls and I head over to one of the boys' dorms. We don't have anything but soda and chips, but someone pops in a CD and dims the lights. A boy grabs my waist. Dancing! Oh, dancing is my favorite, but this isn't the folk dancing I'm used to and I don't recognize the music. Because I don't have a TV or listen to anything but classical music or Psalms on a regular basis, my ears and eyes are desperately tuned in to anything modern or shiny. I hear snatches of phrases and feel the music, raw and untamed: *"Oh, I burn for you..."* Def Leppard's "Animal" is simultaneously horrible and delicious. My body is reacting like I have no say; I am slippery-wet and can feel myself about to climax just from this music, my imagination, my need, and another human pressed against me. The boy and I push away at the same time. I feel my hands and legs tremble. He looks terrified and disappears. Easy come, easy go.

Back at home, my stepfather is trying harder. The change comes after a certain Sunday sermon about the dangers of grounding your children too much. It's so on the nose that I have to wonder if it's aimed at our family specifically.

Doug preaches that the need to form a close connection with your children is "paramount." If they feel close to you, if they feel an unshakable bond, they will be more likely to keep the pattern of excellence and godliness going when they are grown. "Obedience born of love and a desire to please is more powerful than obedience because of the rod alone," Doug states grandly.

So my stepfather starts taking me out for dinner. I stop going after just the second dinner date because we are mistaken for a couple one too many times. Sure, I look like a woman, he is only two years younger than my mom - making him 15 when I was born - and is tall and slender with a full head of dark hair, but ick, no thank you. Instead, we start going back to the school after hours. He lets us in with his keys to watch movies in the school library and I am delighted by this turn of events. What a treat! Even though the movies are old fashioned, he has good taste; *Cyrano De Bergerac* quickly becomes one of my favorites.

I am reading the newspaper one day when I see an ad for the local Miss Junior pageant at the public high school. It states anyone who was a junior in high school is welcome to join.

"That's me!" I think. So I apply. Why not? There is scholarship money to win, and it looks like it could be fun. I know nothing of the pageant world, but I am excited to get a taste. No one from our school has ever entered.

I fill out all the forms, pay the entrance fee, make my way down to the local photographer to get a headshot, and turn it all in. The race is on. I don't tell anyone what I'm doing until I have to. I get a few odd looks, but no one stops me.

I borrow a formal dress from Lila. For my talent, I memorize a sad poem written by a girl from my school. Nothing could have prepared me for the girls I am up against.

There is Christy, who drives a shiny Mustang and has a professional coach training her on all things pageantry. And Anna has a boyfriend and talks about how she spends the night at his house, where they light candles and turn on music before they "make love."

"You sleep with him in the house while his parents are there?!" I squeak. "You sleep in the same bed?!"

All ten shiny heads swivel towards me at the same time and I see confusion and disgust on their faces. I've learned to keep my mouth shut, but just because I've learned doesn't mean I'm good at it. We can't all excel at everything, and keeping my mouth shut is a subject in which I only manage a C at best.

Being around these girls is like being with Scott all over again. I'm thrilled by the opportunity, but it's clear they don't like me and are not at all shy about sharing their feelings. I'm overwhelmed. Overwhelm feels like a cacophony of noise and pressure. My voice gets louder, my thoughts scatter. I want to have fun, to release the anxiety. This doesn't do much to help me stay under the radar.

I get a coveted invite to a sleepover with the girls and it turns into such a hazing that I end up spending the night alone, counting down the hours for it to be over. My makeup bag is tiny compared to the others, my mascara is basic Cover Girl, and I don't have a skin care routine, which is apparently a crucial skill the girls have somehow already mastered. I'm lost, so far behind.

My talent is lame, and my flexibility during the physical excellence routine is sub-par. I keep doing my best, smiling and nodding to make it seem like everything is going according to plan, but my smile is somewhat genuine as I take a secret satisfaction in being so different. I don't do things like everyone else. I don't count calories or eat low fat; I keep the mayo on my McChicken. Even though I am constantly dismayed by my inability to fit in anywhere I go, I'm starting to learn that there is a distinct part of me that likes to go it alone and show everyone up.

There are 11 girls total and three categories to win, with a runner up and a winner for each. To my great pride and astonishment, I win the evening gown category in my borrowed dress for grace and poise. During that particular dance routine, I had smiled so much my cheeks actually ached and I had to massage them after. My parents aren't here to celebrate my accomplishment, but several people from my school showed up to cheer me on, and from this point forward, there will always be a Logos girl in the public pageant.

It's finally my senior year and it is about time. I schedule the same photographer who took my headshot for the pageant and I pay him to take my senior photos. I want both black and white and color photos, which is not cheap but completely worth it. He spends five hours on the photoshoot. He laughs at me when I say I want a black and white shot with a fan blowing my hair across my face, but that picture turns out to be the one he blows up into a poster size and hangs on the front window of his studio. For my school wall, I hand in a color portrait of me in an off-the-shoulder black dress with white polka dots.

As a senior, I try out for and get the lead in the school play. I get to be Ms. Brooks in Our Ms. Brooks and Mr. Callihan volunteers to play opposite me as my love interest. He and the principal, who is always the director of the plays, are good friends and they both agree there isn't a single male student suited for the role. I think it's a little strange but I trust and adore Mr. Callihan. He is our favorite teacher after all.

6

Mr. Callihan

"He was such a magnificent poet he couldn't be bothered with love."

Mr. Callihan paces the floor in front of us as he teaches; our classes with him are in lecture format. Over the years the classroom style, born largely of the fact there are only six of us, has morphed into a free form conversation where we ask questions, bring relevance to modern day, read aloud, and discuss and debate the text. It is my favorite time of the day.

"His wife became despondent because of this," Mr. Callihan continues. "She wanted to attract his attention. She wanted to have his children, but he couldn't be bothered."

"Pfffttt," I respond, oh so eloquently. "It's not that hard to get a man's attention. I would be able to for sure."

I toss my hair, certain of my capabilities in this department. For heaven's sake, a woman would have to be made of dirt to not be able to draw a man's eye. Mr. Callihan seems overcome by this statement. He sits down for a minute to catch his composure, chuckling and stroking his mustache.

"Jade," he says, making an effort to be stern. "You will need to be married very early. You're definitely ready, ripe." The word "ripe" was almost under his breath.

Mr. Callihan had been acting strange lately. It had started with him calling me at home and asking if I would be his teacher's aid during my free period. He then asked my stepfather if he could pick me up for school so I didn't have to walk. I have to be there at a different time than my sister, so I often walk. I feel awkward in the car alone with him, even though it is a short drive.

In his classroom during my free period, I expect to do some sort of work for him, to grade papers, sort something? Instead, he shuts his classroom door and we just talk. Throughout the weeks, his stories become more personal. I listen in fascination, utilizing all my intelligent listening skills; the same ones I had offered Cody the day I compared him to a rock and struck a chord.

I love Mr. Callihan. He is an excellent teacher. He is a deacon in the church and a friend of Doug Wilson's and my stepfather. He is brilliant. I've read some of his poetry and short stories and they are well written. He is old-man-attractive, tall and slim with broad shoulders and an epic mustache. His voice hypnotizes me, low and vibrant. He doesn't make me slippery-wet or swoony; he is just a smart, trustworthy authority figure, one of the only in my life who I am willing to listen to and consider.

So I listen. He tells me about being newly married back in college as he got his Masters, and falling in love with his devastatingly intelligent professor. She would take him to her house where they would smoke pot, talk about the great works, and "sleep together." He feels badly about it, truly, and knows it was a sin, so he stopped long ago and is trying very hard to be attracted to his wife, a good and kind woman, a wonderful mother. He has three little girls and plans to fill his quiver with more.

He's sitting at his desk and I'm leaning over from the opposite side. I've brought my senior photos into class to show Sarah and Kari, and he's asked to see them too. In front of the whole class, he studies the photos carefully, giving each a one-word tribute, like "pensive" or "sultry." He's good at it so I giggle and lean in further.

His voice gets low and husky. "I've been writing a lot of poetry lately. It's like I've been struck by a muse."

"Oh! Let me read it, please? Wait." I pause. "Is it about me?"

"Some of it, yes."

"Ok, give it over." I'm titillated. I can't help it.

"Maybe, maybe some of it. But not right now. What I've written wouldn't be appropriate for you to read."

A strand of my long hair brushes against his knuckles and his whole body fills with air as he sits back. I turn and walk back to my desk. The rest of the class has stayed mostly quiet, pretending not to watch our interaction.

Mr. Callihan sometimes comes into Pizza Hut where I work and drinks coffee and reads or grades papers. One night, there's a particularly large and rowdy group of college guys and they flirt with me, amazed at how many sodas I can carry at a time, how fast I can serve their pan pizza, whistling every time I turn to walk away. I just grin and laugh with them, telling them they'd better tip me really well since they're so difficult to deal with.

I'm closing so it's late, nearly 1 am, when I finally get to my car. It won't start. I try again, panicking. The restaurant doors are already locked so I don't have a way to call my mom.

Out of the darkness, Mr. Callihan emerges from his car a few yards away, scaring me to death when he materializes at my window.

"Your car won't start, will it?" he asks, knowingly.

"No!" I answer with a nervous laugh. "I have no idea why. It was fine before! Why are you still here anyway?" Has he been sitting in his car for hours, just waiting for me? That was...nice of him. He's so protective.

"I had a feeling those guys were going to hurt you in some way and wanted to protect you. You were so forward with them, you encouraged them, flirted with them. Sure enough, I saw them messing with your car when they came out. I'm sure I scared them away. Pop your hood for me."

I do and he disappears to the front of my car and comes back less than two minutes later.

"Try again," he says, softly. My car starts right away.

"Oh my goodness! How did you do that?" I exclaim. "I don't know what I would have done if you hadn't been here."

I'm relieved, but anxious and confused at the thought of those happy go lucky boys damaging my car purposefully and then running away to leave me stranded.

"This is a good lesson for you." He grabs my left hand with both of his, looking at me imploringly. "Be careful what impression you leave on men.

If you give them an inch they will take a mile."

This interaction kickstarts a series of rather unfortunate events during the last months of school. The first is when he professes his love and proposes to me as Mr. Boynton on stage during the *Our Ms Brooks* production. During the last show, I see a tear trickling down his cheek in the stage lights. I'm suddenly relieved the play is over; there has been way too much hand holding and gazing into one another's eyes for my comfort.

At the end of the year, we watch a movie in Kari's basement for our class party. I'm frozen in place as the all too familiar *The Princess Bride* plays on the screen. We all have it memorized as it's one of the only modern movies deemed intelligent and appropriate enough to be endorsed at Logos, but all I can focus on is Mr. Callihan's hands. He keeps reaching back and caressing my leg in the dark, squeezing my calf and thigh gently but insistently. His hands feel good - who doesn't like a rub down? But I'm sure everyone else can see. Josh keeps twitching uncomfortably beside me.

But things really come to a head when our class collectively chooses Mr. Callihan to speak at our graduation and to be one of our chaperones for our class trip in Seattle. He calls me one night when Sarah is sleeping over.

"I want you to know I'm going to ride my motorcycle to Seattle instead of taking the van with all of you," he says, his breath hitching. "I'm doing this because I want you to ride with me. I will need to give everyone a turn but I'm doing it for you. Jade. There's a list of qualities that make a woman desirable, the ultimate woman. You don't just check every box on that list. You ARE the list."

Well, my young heart is thrilled. This seems epic. I'm not sure I'm ready to be a woman, but I'm a few short weeks from turning 18 so it sort of makes sense. My heart is racing and I tell Sarah about the phone call. When I finish, we look at each other lamely. I see sadness and confusion on her face and fear fills her eyes, or maybe that all belongs to me and she's a mirror. I want this story to be about a guy, any guy. But not Mr. Callihan.

A few weeks later, we're listening to Mr. Callihan read a Ray Bradbury story when he pauses dramatically.

"Dreams can be so strange, can't they?" he begins, thoughtfully. "It can be tempting to give them more meaning than they deserve. For instance, the other night I had a dream about you, Jade. You were sitting at a table. I think it was a dining room table because of the light fixture above you, and you were licking an envelope like you were going to seal it. Strange isn't it?"

My entire body freezes.

"When?" I ask, stunned. "When did you have that dream about me?"

"Hmmm, it was two nights ago I think. Yes, two nights ago."

"I was doing that two nights ago!" I nearly squeal with delight. This is a shiver-worthy miracle. The class and Mr. Callihan look at me in disbelief.

"No, I swear!" I insist. "Two nights ago I was writing a letter to my cousin Jason. I was sitting at my dining room table. The envelope wasn't sealing so I had to keep licking it." I giggle.

Mr. Callihan looks at me searchingly for about 15 seconds and then continues to guide the discussion. I'm in shock. We are truly connected if he's seeing me in his dreams doing something I ACTUALLY did.

A few weeks later is my graduation party, which we've planned in conjunction with my 18th birthday. It seems obvious to invite Mr. Callihan. The weather is beautiful so we open all the windows and set things up in the backyard. There are a lot of people here, with cards and presents everywhere. The sun is shining and I feel loved.

When Mr. Callihan arrives, I grab his hand and pull him over to my mother who is standing in the dining room.

"Mom!" I'm so excited to tell this story I can barely contain myself. "A few weeks ago Mr. Callihan had a dream about me sitting at this table and licking an envelope. You know when I was writing that letter to Jason?" I keep babbling but my voice trails off. Mr. Callihan looks deeply uncomfortable and embarrassed. My mom is frozen. I follow her eyes to the line of trees that edge our backyard. Unease fills my body, but I don't know what it means, and I'm not sure what to say, so I change the subject and laugh loudly.

We all chat for a few more awkward moments and Mr. Callihan leaves almost as soon as he arrives. He presents me with a second edition in two volumes of *The Count of Monte Cristo*, one of my favorite books. Inscribed on the flyleaf are the words, "Jade, please enjoy. There are so few men like the Count anymore. - Wes."

The day of our class trip arrives and I am first on the bike behind Mr. Callihan. I will admit, riding on the back of this motorcycle is one of the yummiest things I've done since flying up on the hay elevator. I feel the motor vibrating and Mr. Callihan revs it occasionally, swerving just a bit so I have to tighten my thighs and arms around him. I get all but the last hour or so of the five-hour trip to Seattle, a fact I hear Jon complaining bitterly about at the gas station. My classmates look at me accusingly; I feel separate from them, apart, and it doesn't feel good anymore.

That night, the six of us stay up in one hotel room, drinking too much soda and laughing until we cry. This feels even better to me than riding behind Mr. Callihan. I don't want to be his chosen one any longer. The connection I have with him is real so I know I can trust him and that he'll understand my truth.

The next day, I'm perched behind him on the bike yet again as we follow the van on our way back to the hotel from Pike Street Market. I take a deep breath when we get to a stoplight, my voice conveniently muffled by the helmet.

"I liked it better when we were just friends."

I feel his body stiffen. He keeps his eyes straight ahead, his voice barely audible over the rumble of the motor.

"What did you say?"

"I said I liked it better when we were just friends. I just want to be your friend."

"I understand." That's all he says, and I know he truly does understand. I'm sure he must feel the same. He's not my teacher anymore, we crossed that boundary long ago, and I'm a graduate now. I'm 18. He can be my friend. I will keep his secrets safe. Anything my body is telling me beyond that I ignore. When in doubt, just float up.

The next morning our second chaperone tells us Mr. Callihan has left.

"He had a family emergency," is all she says.

The remaining two days are a blur. I can no longer focus, and spend the bulk of the time disconnected, watching my body go through the motions from a safe distance.

I am home for an hour or maybe a day before my stepfather empties the trailer of children and tells me to sit down. There is a fury rising from his body; the heat is palpable, I can feel it radiating off of him. The pit of my stomach knows this is about Mr. Callihan. I cannot comprehend the words that are said to me in the next 20 minutes. I only hear snippets. I have become a wild rabbit shocked into stillness by a sudden movement, a noise, certain that it can't be seen and killed if it stays perfectly frozen.

Lost in the nothingness I hear, "You will go to hell if you continue this path." I hear "seductress," do I hear "whore?" Mr. Sample's prediction has come true. I am nothing more than the woman Proverbs warned about time and time again: *"For the lips of an immoral woman drip honey, And her mouth is smoother than oil; But in the end she is bitter as wormwood, Sharp as a two-edged sword. Her feet go down to death, Her steps lay hold of hell."*

My stepfather has tried so hard to mold and shape and train me, but now he says he's giving up. He doesn't know what to do with me. I have learned nothing. He's giving me over to my wickedness.

I am called into Doug Wilson's office next. He is much gentler, even jovial at times, and tries to make me comfortable as he reads me the error of my unintentional ways. Again, I leave my body and only hear snatches of what's transpiring.

It's been one week since the senior trip. Tomorrow is Sunday and Mr. Callihan will be at church with the rest of us. I will have to see him tomorrow and look him in the face. I am so embarrassed and confused.

"Jade, you're no mud fence," Doug states with certainty. A picture of a muddy, dirty fence springs to my mind. I'm not a mud fence, I'm better than that. An attractive fence, white picket maybe. Okay, I'm tracking, I think.

"See," he continues. "We've always known you were going to have trouble with boys. And we're just glad something like this has happened under our watch so we can guide and direct you, show you how a woman needs to behave with a man."

What? What has happened under their watch? The rest of his words may as well be in Greek, perhaps they really are. Many of the men in our community, including my stepfather, study Greek and Hebrew so they can read the Bible in its original languages.

I do in fact see Mr. Callihan the next day at church. I'm coming out of the bathroom and there he is. He looks brokenhearted, dejected, and stares forlornly at me.

"Hi," I stammer. "Are you okay?"

He looks down and shakes his head sadly.

"Are we still going to be able to be friends?" I ask, suddenly struck with the fact that one of the most constants in my life, my daily interaction with Mr. Callihan, might be changing forever. He's told my stepfather and Doug Wilson the whole truth, confessed, and I have been found as the guilty one.

"No. No, Jade. We can't be friends." Mr. Callihan's voice is barely above a whisper. He gazes at me one last time and walks away.

To the Outside Girl, with Love

My love, you watch others watching you.

You hold your breath and wait to see what they might think.

You become them, see with their eyes, and thus the very core of you cannot be trusted, cannot be tolerated.

But I will tell you what I see.

I am Kalaratri, destroyer of darkness and ignorance.

I am cloaked by the night, and use its cover to destroy any warriors who violate the rules of law.

My child, do you hear me wailing?

The sounds that emanate from my belly would turn those men to stone, petrified by the horror of what they know I will do to them.

I am truth witnessed and laid bare.

I am the dark night of the soul, the dark night of final dissolution, of that which no longer needs to be.

Wait for me.

I am coming.

IV

Adulting

They say silence is golden, but there's a lot of wealthy women who can't buy their own freedom.

7

If You Can't Be With the One You Love, Honey, Love the One You're With

I bury myself in waiting tables at Pizza Hut for the summer. I'm also planning to go to the U of I in the fall. My stepfather says I can continue to live in the trailer rent free and that will be my parents' contribution to college. Boys and men alike continue to try and land on me. I'm a pile of cow dung and they can't seem to stop buzzing. I bat them away, too exhausted to fathom navigating a relationship in my current state of shame.

My sister Mary is about to start her second year of high school and has become hip and cute. She's an amazing writer with a solid group of friends who manage to have opinions without being targeted, and if they are, they gather collectively to stand up for themselves, even if it's just to write snarky haikus about their teachers or smash the holier than thou students in debates.

Mary is wise beyond her years. One afternoon we're out running errands and I find myself pouring out my words about Mr. Callihan, explaining what happened, how badly I messed up. No one has asked me my version of events so I've never explained anything out loud and I'm finding some relief in verbally processing. When I'm finally done, Mary sits quietly. She hasn't said much of anything except for a few generally comforting phrases like, "That's messed up, Jade. This doesn't make any sense. Wow, that's so heavy." I know my sister well enough to understand that though she's overwhelmed by the information, she's already processing and we are far from finished with this subject matter.

Yet I start to move on. I'm back to living 90% of my life as a safe observer from above, hovering just outside my body. Outwardly I laugh and smile. I brazenly flirt now, desperate for connection.

First there's Gary, the morose cook who teaches at the U of I and works at Pizza Hut in the summers. He tells me about his travels, details from all the places in the world he's been. I tell him I want to go to Greece someday. "I'll take you to Greece," he replies, nonchalantly.

"You will?" I laugh. "What would we do there?"

"We would play in the sand and sun all day, and I would make love to you every night." I'm a sucker for poetic discourse, and very nearly agree to run away with him right then and there.

Then there's a new cook, ironically named David, who lets me know upfront that he's started working there because he met me as a customer. He asks me on a date right away.

"No," I say. "No, I can't date you because you're not a Christian."

"How do you know what I am?" he parries. Good point.

"Well, are you? Are you a Christian? Have you given your life to Jesus?"

He shakes his head and laughs. "I'm always searching. Tell me more."

So now I'm preaching the gospel day in and day out to this boy who is four years older than me. He's very receptive. I introduce him to Doug and he starts going to see him on a regular basis. He's immediately smitten with this brand of Christianity and loves the rules, regulations, and path to clean living with the promise of cultural domination.

Things between us escalate quickly. We're officially dating because he's a full-fledged Christian now. His ardor and intensity make me uncomfortable, but I'm too desensitized to care.

One day I'm waiting for him at the mall, annoyed because he's so late, when I finally see him walking towards me. I start to complain but then see his knees are covered in blood, his hand and elbow, clothes too. I take in his appearance with horror.

"I got into a bike accident on the way here," he explains. "It was pretty bad."

"Why are you HERE right now?" I ask. "You must be in so much pain. You need to clean all of that up!"

"I'm here because I gave you my word that I would come. I keep my word."

Another time, he's pushing me in a swing and I call back to him to go higher. He trips on his way under the swing attempting an underdog and falls flat on his face. His look of disgust at himself for messing up, his need to make it right and try again and again makes me laugh, but with unease. He's a lot.

To get him off my scent and shake myself free, I decide to tell him about Mr. Callihan. I weave the story carefully, making sure he understands that I'm damaged goods, absolutely not to be trusted, a harlot of sorts. This backfires in a magnificent way. He is shocked and astonished.

"This guy has been fired, right?" he exclaims.

"No, no, why would he be?" I respond.

He explains that I couldn't possibly be at fault because I was the student, he was the teacher. That it doesn't matter what I've done, only that Mr. Callihan has broken the student-teacher trust. He is culpable. I had never considered this perspective and I'm not sure how to feel about it. He kisses me, tells me he is so sorry that this horrible thing has happened, and that he wants to protect me. I suppose I should feel safe and cared for now.

Just a few days after this interaction, Mary tells me that she couldn't keep my story about Mr. Callihan a secret and she had to do something about it. She's told one of her best friends, Laura, who went directly to her dad. Their family belongs to Jim Wilson's church and they ask me to come over immediately.

I do what I'm told and find myself in yet another living room with Jim Wilson. This time, it's me doing the talking instead of waiting in another room. Jim is the first person to ask me for my version of the events. I tell him everything. I don't hold back or weave the story, I stick to the facts. He asks me questions and I answer. The more I speak, the more I come into my body, feeling the relief of simply being asked to share my words. Jim is not one to wait around for the 'right thing to be done,' this I know, but I'm still surprised when he borrows the phone and tells his son, Doug, to come to the family's house right away.

Doug and Jim are in another room for a while. I'm sitting in the living room, not exactly sure why I'm still there, when they emerge. Doug says nothing to me, he barely glances my way, but when he does look at me, it's with a naked rage I can see in his eyes.

I'm encouraged to tell my story again, this time to Tom Garfield, my longtime principal and director at Logos, who happens to be a good friend of Mr. Callihan. David is by my side for moral support.

Mr. Garfield looks at me quizzically when I'm finished, a rueful smile on his lips. "Why didn't you say all of this months ago?"

"Because no one asked me!" I exclaim. "Because Mr. Callihan came to all of you and told you everything, so I figured you already knew."

"My dear," Mr. Garfield begins somberly. "That is not the version we were told. Mr. Callihan is a godly man and an amazing teacher. It's a pity he won't be able to be part of the faculty any longer."

Mr. Callihan isn't fired but he does "step down to pursue another line of education." His place in the community, in the church, remains secure. I tell myself justice has been served, while not at all being sure that I understand what that means. I just know that the shame and guilt is like a gag, so thick it chokes me.

Six months after meeting him, I say yes to David's repeated desire to make me his wife, his many promises of protection. He is earnest and believable, if his support through my experience with Mr. Callihan is any indication, and right now I'm living in a trailer with my stepdad who will not relinquish his duty and responsibility to keep me pure until he hands me over to my husband. I figure my odds are better with David the boy than David the man.

This is the way I prove myself. I am ripe. I am blooming and lush. I am headed to hell as a seductress with honeyed lips, but if I marry, I will prove my obedience to God's ways and have protection.

We plan the wedding for June 1st. We even have sex. I think. Actually, he has to tell me that's what it was. My version of events is we were giving each other massages on the floor and he kept asking me if it was okay. I kept saying yes, but I didn't feel much of anything. I don't feel much nowadays, though. So now I am no longer a virgin, I've had sex before marriage. This is a serious sin. Add it to the funeral pyre.

We reset the clock and vow to stay away from one another sexually until the wedding. I buy the first dress I try on and pay for it with tips. David and I are paying for the wedding ourselves so we use the Logos school auditorium for the reception to cut costs. Creamy white and dark green is one of my favorite color combos, so we cut countless stems of ivy and thread them through a white trellis; it looks like a dreamy white picket fence. My grandma makes the bridesmaid's dresses to go with my color palette of forest green and ashes of roses pink. Ashes of roses is a nod to one of my favorite books, *The Thorn Birds*, and, like Meggie, I know I've unwittingly tempted an older, godly man to sin. My marriage is a penance of sorts.

In addition to my sister Mary, I ask Sarah to be in my wedding party. Though we've never spoken in depth about what happened to me, I feel she knows the most of anyone in our class and understands. David's mother, dismayed that her oldest son has fallen in with religion, is the only adult to express concern about our age and the speed of our engagement. She questions how we will live, where we will live. She implores us to wait until we're finished with college. David tells her that we could never live in sin and can't wait a moment longer.

The wedding is beautiful and goes off without a hitch. Doug Wilson marries us. My headband style veil, thick with fake pearls, arrives the morning of the wedding and I put it on and keep it there, despite the vice-like grip that gives me a raging headache. Countless people tell me I'm the most beautiful bride they've ever seen. I nod and smile so wide I have to massage my cheeks. I am winning another round of presence and composure, but inside I have returned to my wild rabbit state. I want to run but I am frozen. I want to tear off the veil and scream. I have a deep longing to teleport, to disappear without explanation, maybe run away to Greece with Gary.

Our honeymoon, a quick trip to Coeur d' Alene, is one of the loneliest times of my life. I cry in the dark while we have sex. David doesn't know because I don't kiss and tell. I smile and wave, ever the perfect pageant girl. My frozen rabbit state stays hidden. I will always win this category.

I have been 19 years old for two months.

We live in the basement of David's aunt's bookstore for almost nothing. There's no kitchen but we make do. Every morning David wakes up, happy to be alive and beside me, and touches my body, pets my hair, whispers in my ear, and I just want to kill him. I am so angry I hit him sometimes, and he retreats in sorrow and anger. I even punch him in my sleep once and give him a bloody nose.

David says we need spiritual marriage counseling from a pastor or elder. We are told to have babies as soon as possible, a fact I already knew from being a member of Doug's church for so long. The most important purpose of a verdant woman is to make babies; it grows God's kingdom and keeps the marriage on track, keeps the woman's gaze downward, and ignites her biological need to be a nurturer. Use it or lose it.

David and I have epic fights. We both hate condoms and I'm allergic to the latex, and despite the church's recommendation to make babies immediately, I'm unwilling to take responsibility for another life. I'm not even sure I want to have children, so I go on birth control, and it makes me feel crazy. I scream and cry out, wander around in our tiny backyard in the night, I even hallucinate a few times. David punches a hole in the wall with rage. He thinks about packing a bag and leaving but returns to me, saying he will never leave. He gave a vow to God and he will never break it. When I am mad he holds me tightly and won't let me leave his iron grip until I give in, but his definition of giving in means I collapse in tears and let him hold me. I learn to knock on each door before I enter a room, even tap on the wall as I approach him, because if he's startled even a bit he will move like lightning towards the noise, and land with his fist near my face, ready to vanquish the danger. I decide that all my mental issues are due to the birth control pills, so I stop taking them and use a spermicide foam instead, resigned to the fact that it's only 80% effective.

Eventually, I receive a call from Jim Nance, my old high school teacher, who is an elder at our church. He's checking in on how things are going, asking me how he can pray for me, how our marriage is thriving, and how David is treating me.

"Oh!" I say. "We're good, thank you for asking. We're so good. David loves me so much and is incredibly kind and patient with me." I laugh nervously. "As you know, I can be a bit of a handful but he treats me with such care."

Mr. Nance murmurs his congratulations and throws out a few "praise God"s. When I hang up, I walk robot-like to the bathroom and stare at myself in the tiny mirror. My choices are clear. I can stay in this marriage and be miserable, or I can stay in this marriage and be happy. I refuse to be miserable. I look myself in the eye and sternly repeat over and over, "You have made this bed, *you* have made this bed, and now you have to lie in it." And lie I will.

If marriage is the only place I can safely scratch my itch, I am determined to do so. We start having sex constantly. I know how to finish and it's even better with a penis than when I take care of myself, though I do plenty of that too despite it being a sin. I instinctively know how to get on top, how to turn around, how to get on all fours. But I will not let his mouth anywhere near my vagina. I will not suck on his penis. I get mad at him if he finishes before I do. This is supposed to be fun for both of us.

I make a scavenger hunt for David's birthday. I let him pick out a parka I hate and wear it to keep me warm while I walk to class. We hike to Domino's with a paper bag to grab pizza and keep it hot, pick up Bud Light Ice on the way back, and watch movies. We hang out like roommates and have sex like rabbits.

My cousin Jason is now attending the U of I as well and living in the dorms. We're together all the time. He's still my best friend. We talk about everything so I tell him all about the joys of being able to have sex. It's a great reason to get married, I say. He laughs.

The truth is that I prefer his company to David's. I love him more than I love David. I am more attracted to him than I am to David and feel more free to be myself. It feels horrible to admit so I never come right out and say it, but Jason and I know each other so well there's no hiding it. I'm in his dorm room constantly. We talk and laugh or sit in silence and do homework. We're obsessed with U2 and listen to our *Rattle and Hum* and *Achtung Baby* CDs on repeat. He lets me sleep on his chest, or turns music on and watches me dance. He won't ever make a move and neither will I. I am married. We never even say I love you.

I drive south with him to visit his family. It's one of the best road trips of my life. We sleep together on his bed at night and I can feel his need. He's never given in to it but on this night I want him to. I move his hand and slip it under my shirt, towards my breast and his breath hitches.

"No. No Jade. We can't. If I start I will never stop. Do you understand?"

I do understand. I head home the next day with a heaviness in my chest and doom in the air.

David has caught on to my preference. His jealousy is understandable. He knows I respect Jim Wilson, so he makes me go with him to get counseling about the situation. Jim talks to us for some time. He asks many questions. He is somber and predictably insistent that whatever needs to be taken care of be taken care of immediately. He tells me, with David nodding emphatically in the background, that I will call Jason as soon as we get home and tell him I will never see him again, except at family functions. I start to cry and say that Jason will never understand, never forgive me.

"Is there anything Jason knows about, regarding the two of you, that he could use against you?" Jim asks.

David and I look at each other.

"He knows- he knows we had sex before we were married," I stammer.

David's eyes breathe fire in my direction.

"This is very serious," Jim replies. "It's extremely important that you tell your father, Jade, before Jason retaliates."

We drive home in icy silence. As soon as we arrive, David hands me the phone.

"Call him," he says. "Call him and then let's do damage control for this situation you've created."

My call to Jason is done with my soul at a safe distance from my body, observing in horror. Jason asks me questions. At first he's incredulous and then he starts crying too. I've never heard him cry before.

"I came to you first Jason," I say woodenly. "I came to you before I got married and you didn't tell me to stop. You didn't want me. David wants me." When I hang up the phone, I am so empty I have no tears to cry.

Though it's clear to me there will be no retaliation, David insists we tell my stepfather and my mother of our transgression. My stepfather's reaction is naturally one of disgust and horror, nothing new there.

Jason's mother, sweet Anne, hears about the scandal and calls me on the phone to ask me why I'm doing this to her son, to our family. Her voice breaks as she tells me how much I've hurt Jason. I only manage to say that I'm following my husband's wishes, and that I never meant any harm.

I've only finished my first year of college, but David is about to graduate with his teaching degree and is offered a well paid position in Boise for the summer. I convince him, no small task, to go and live with his mom, where he can work and save money for us, and to let me stay in Moscow because I've just landed a job waiting tables at the nicest hotel restaurant in town.

I was sick of Pizza Hut, and I chose this place because I was certain I could make more money and smell less like hot oil. Here, interesting people show up here from all over the world. We wear skirts and blouses, or button up shirts, bowties, and slacks, fold the napkins into pyramids, and open the wine at the customer's table. Just as I had when I was 16, I walked in and announced that I was here for the job. The manager first offered me a hostess or busser position, explaining that's where everyone starts but I detailed my years of experience and batted my eyes to snag a waitress spot instead. This makes me the target of every other girl there and the backlash is intense, partially because I bypassed the pecking order, but also because the frozen rabbit that is part of my psyche is always with me. It feels like a strange glitch; I behave and learn normally and then forget something obvious, or misplace something important, or break something expensive. This has happened my entire life. My manager at Pizza Hut called me both the best and the worst waitress he'd ever managed in his 15 years. By the time David needs to leave for Boise, I am just starting to settle in and there's no way I'm leaving my cushy job to live with his mother for the summer.

Within weeks of David being gone, I am a new woman. I become obsessed with jazzercise and resistance training and now I fit into my skinniest jeans most appealingly. I am so happy to have my own space, to make my own choices. I haven't had my own bedroom since I was five and I relish it. I go dancing every Friday and Saturday. I almost have sex with a visiting comedian in my car, but make him stop when I realize he's putting on a condom to do the deed. His is only the second penis I've seen as a woman, and I am both shocked by the sheer size of it and horrified at how much I want to try it on. I get roofied at a house party, feeling mouths and hands on my body, but manage to drag myself to Robert's room, a co-worker I feel safe with. I climb into his bed, he follows me, and through my haze I beg him to protect me. I get drunk after a sunny day spent at the dunes and spend the night at a stranger's house. I keep myself from having sex with anyone, but I am still having the time of my life, though I am also riddled with guilt and shame at behaving like a hussy. Robert becomes obsessed with protecting me and drunkenly serenades me every night outside my window.

A few days before David returns home, I make Robert solemnly swear to never come near my house again. I clean the basement thoroughly, and stay, nun-like, in its cramped quarters until he arrives. I do my best to purge my wild ways, but David can sense that something's shifted within me.

We are both in agreement that something has to change. I bravely admit to him that I don't feel safe in Doug Wilson's church. I know that I'm supposed to be pro-Doug, but all I can see when I look at him is his rage for my having been the reason his wishes, his decree, was bypassed. I hear his voice telling me, in so many words, that it was my fault, and that I'm "no mud fence."

We move back to Boise together this time, but David insists we still listen to Doug's recorded sermons every Sunday until we find a proper church. We move into a small apartment half a mile from the high school where David will be teaching. I start attending BSU, teaching aerobics, and I get a job waiting tables at Outback Steakhouse. I get straight As. I open a Betty Crocker cookbook that we received as a wedding gift and I learn to cook. I keep myself so busy that it becomes a form of happiness.

But at least once a day, I continue to look in the mirror and remind myself, "You made this bed, now you will lie in it." I tell myself that this is true happiness.

Our friends Matt and Holly come for a visit. Holly had been a year below me at Logos and had also brought a recruit to the church and married him straight out of high school. Matt is as enthusiastic as David about his newfound religion but I sense that Holly is not as happy and it makes me deeply uncomfortable. It's too close to home, this unhappiness.

A couple of days into their visit, Holly tells me something is wrong. They've been to marriage counseling with Doug and have been told they need to have a baby. Holly almost cries when she tells me that she can barely bring herself to have sex with him, partly because he can barely bring himself to have sex with her, and partly because when he does express interest, he wants to do strange things with her body. She can't begin to think about making a baby with him. I tell her that sex is the fun part, that she should keep trying to keep Matt happy and not worry about the rest. I sneak into the kitchen in the middle of the night, desperate for a drink of water, and hear Holly trying to do just that.

Holly leaves Matt not long after. She is ostracized from her family and the church community in Moscow. I cannot fathom this treatment of her. I've spent countless nights at her house as a teen and know how close she is to both her parents, to her siblings, and how much they love her. There is kindness in their family. But rules are rules. She is living in sin now, excommunicated, and until she repents and goes back to her husband, she must be treated as an outsider.

Outwardly I gossip and *tsk* with David about the situation, inwardly I am terrified and cling tighter to the rules for absolution.

David's need to constantly judge himself and others exhausts me. I repeatedly ask him to stop talking about everyone, putting them down, begging him to be happy with what he has, but contentment seems to elude him.

I've been married for two years and David talks in circles about all the children we're going to have. I just laugh it off and shake my head. The truth is I have no desire to have a baby but also know that the quiver-filling is inevitable. David and I have both continued to listen to Doug's sermons, read his books, and feel the pressure all the way from Moscow. At the same time, I figure there's no way I'm fertile; all we use is spermicide foam right before David finishes, so I stop using it consistently.

My friend Trish comes to visit. She is my only non-Christian friend; I met her at my hotel restaurant job. She often kept me safe in the debauchery of my David-less summer. She's also pregnant with our old manager's baby, the same one who let me skip straight to server. She apologizes for being so tired, begs for McDonald's, and complains about her breasts being tender. I nap with her because I'm tired too, I chomp down McDonald's with enthusiasm, and realize my breasts are sore to the touch. She laughs and tells me I should take a pregnancy test.

It's positive. I'm 21 years old.

8

Lessons in Love

We don't have health insurance, but David receives a small inheritance when his grandmother passes and it pays, almost to the penny, for a birth at the birthing center in nearby Nampa. Anything beyond the birth, any meds or complications that cause me to go to the hospital across the street, will be out of pocket. I'm determined to stay within the budget in every area of my life. I park off campus and walk the mile to classes, I keep waiting tables and teaching aerobics. I don't tell anyone I'm pregnant, which isn't too difficult as almost no one on campus even knows I'm married.

When I'm seven months along it becomes impossible to hide: my body stays its normal size but my stomach is a gigantic beach ball. It begins to sink in that this is going to happen and I dive into the wonder of it. We find out we're having a girl, and I check out a book at the library with a title promising to offer classic baby names that have never been in *or* out of style. I choose Audrey Paige.

We have two bedrooms and I decorate the nursery with a classic Winnie the Pooh theme, only able to afford a few key pieces. I wash all the baby clothes in Dreft and fold them in a second-hand dresser. We live close to David's mom and she is horrified that we're having a baby at such a young age, but we smile and plan and wait.

When Audrey is two weeks late I am finally induced. Determined not to spend another penny, I ride the waves of pitocin without so much as an ibuprofen. In addition, you can't stay overnight at the birthing center or it costs extra money; they give you no more than eight hours to give birth and recover under their care. So I'm up from my bed and showering 30 minutes after having my sweet baby, I make sure she latches to feed, and we are home just three short hours after her birth.

Doug Wilson is right. He knows everything. Having a baby takes all your longings, your energy, your confusion, and laser focuses it on the objective need to keep a tiny human alive. Having a baby reminds you how important, how vital the family unit is, how great God's mercies are.

In my verdant youth, my lush body is fast to bounce back, I have so much milk I can shoot it across a room, I trickle breast milk on my nipples after each feeding and leave them out to air dry so they don't crack, and when they do, I bite my lip and keep going. My entire being is being utilized as God intended.

Audrey is an angel. I write poems about her perfection, I praise God for her tiny fingers and toes, I marvel at how she melts everyone's heart: David, his mother, my mother, my stepfather, my sisters, my brother. I am full of forgiveness for everyone and everything. I know my place in the Kingdom of God.

Then there are the hellish parts. I've torn badly during the birth so I can't poop properly. I go to my doctor six weeks postpartum, determined to get some help. He rushes into the room, lifts my gown, says, "You can resume sexual relations," and scurries off to a C-section.

David gets a new career in sales because he can't see himself teaching forever and we need more money so I don't have to work. The problem is, I love working. Being inside my stuffy apartment with a baby all day, now sans car because David can no longer walk to work, feels claustrophobic. He says I don't need to finish my degree. I can't see a way to do that with a baby anyway and I give it up, only three semesters away from finishing.

I begin to keep a journal where I ask for God's forgiveness for wanting more: more than just the blessings of motherhood, more than the duties of being a wife. I search my mind for mistakes I've made, people I've taken advantage of and write to them or call them - Cody, Josh, some old teachers, my mother - and ask for their forgiveness.

But I don't reach out to Jason. The wound there is too deep, and I have to hold the mirage in place that it is wicked to communicate except during family events. I shut him out of my mind and heart, even when his precious mother passes away and I know he must be crushed. I can feel his devastation in my bones.

We find a duplex with a backyard and a wood burning fireplace closer to the city in a cute neighborhood. I don't have a car but I have neighbors I love, I have the hardest working husband in the world, a new church family, and I am determined to get it right this time.

The next seven years are curated to fit my new paradigm of a woman, the Proverbs 31 woman who "rises when it is yet night and provides food for her household." I have two more daughters with the same precision and organization as my first, even using the same book to name them: Allana Rene and Sophia Grace. My quiver is getting full and my daughters are beautiful, well dressed and obedient, hilarious and bright. I have a journal that I use to carefully catalog their brilliance. I navigate life and find more joy.

I have moderate to severe anemia. Anytime my blood is taken, the doctors exclaim and throw out numbers: "The low end of normal is 12 and you're at 8! You shouldn't be driving." They don't seem to understand I do a lot more than drive in this state, but the iron pills they prescribe upset my system so badly I rarely take them.

There's a tired fog over me most of the time, but it doesn't slow me down - there's too much to do! I start a bookclub where only the classics are chosen. To keep my brain sharp, I often write essays or thesis papers about the books, sometimes sharing them with the group. I make friends with the other mothers of my church and with my neighbor across the street who is a Christian but not of the caliber of a Doug Wilson church, a fact that keeps me from trusting her fully.

Doug's denomination is the Confederation of Reformed Evangelicals, or CREC. We don't have a branch in Boise, so David and I gather with a few other couples to start meeting together, making our own brand of faith utilizing Doug's materials along with teachings from John Piper, Timothy Keller, and the Bible. Always the Bible.

The book most often recommended by Doug and Nancy for child rearing is *To Train Up a Child,* which tells parents to start behavior training before your children can walk. A perfect example is to set them up on a square of blanket and tell them to stay; spank them if they get off. If they seem content on the blanket, tempt them with a toy a few feet away and then spank them for coming after the toy. The rod should be used constantly, all day. Sheer obedience is what the first five years are for, because if they obey now, "when they are older they will not depart from it." I am militant but kind.

"It" of course is The Faith itself. "It" is happiness in the Lord. To find that happiness, I carefully construct what I see, do, and consume. I can't belong to the world. I must control myself. When I hear sappy love songs I scoff; no one actually feels that way. Arranged marriage and formal courtship make sense to me.

I become pragmatic about feelings in general but I still glitch from time to time. Back from my time as the best and worst waitress, that sporadic model continues in adulting. I can manage everything: laundry, homemade meals, a perfectly clean house decorated beautifully on a budget, raising three wonderful children, church fellowship, friendship, hosting, David's countless needs, but I lose everything. I lock my keys in the car while it's running. I forget things so often that Audrey, as early as two years old, starts a litany every time we leave the house. "Mama, do you have your keys? Do you have your wawwet? Did evvybody go to the bafroom?" I laugh at myself for my silly mistakes and airheaded ways. I'm not the sharpest knife in the drawer, but I keep sawin' away.

We finally buy a small but perfect house with vaulted ceilings. There's a creek a block away and I take my girls and we walk for miles, picking wild blackberries along the way. At night I walk by myself and climb trees, needing to be as close to the sky as possible, to feel the wind on my face, and I pray for strength. I have sex with my husband when he wants it. I am thankful.

Managing my children and home is a whole full-time job. Dealing with

David is another. He is in his glory when he's protecting and serving and everyone knows it. Having babies, small children, and a wife who cannot cope without his help is right up his alley. I make most of the decisions for the home, but frame things so that he holds head of household status. His authority, his priest-head in our home, is everything to him. He also bemoans his lot in life so consistently it's like a *drip drip drip* constantly in my ear. He's searching for more too, but my encouragement is mostly met with impossibilities on his end. It's always about not having enough, not being enough. He can't seem to climb any ladder, believing he has no control, that "the man" is always keeping him down. I spend countless hours encouraging him, explaining to him that you receive what you put out, that anything is possible, but it falls on deaf ears.

Leadership within the church feeds David's need to be of service for the Kingdom of God so we join in and help whenever possible. The pastor and worship leader/head elder are brothers with a plethora of personal problems. We attract Doug Wilson and CREC followers and grow to over 100 members.

There's a family here that, like us, keeps having children, but unlike us are not able to manage the load. The mother constantly calls and asks the other mothers for babysitting, for meals, for help cleaning her home. I am so enraged by this I see red. I say no when my help is asked for because I simply don't have the bandwidth.

Her husband approaches me one Sunday and starts up a conversation about the importance of the church family to be in fellowship.

"You are strong," he says in summation. "You are one of the strongest women I've ever met. My wife is weak. The strong need to help the weak."

I am flattered and dismayed at this view of me. I am simply putting one foot in front of the other. I never get enough sleep. I do everything alone. If I can do it, anyone can do it. And they should.

Brought on largely by the bitterness between the brothers, the church implodes. At one of our last services David is up on the stage, fielding questions. Sitting in the audience, I am offended by a particular comment and open my mouth to speak. David puts his finger to his lips and shakes his head at me. I close my mouth. Afterwards, a couple we knew from Doug's church in Moscow rushes to congratulate David. Scott, the husband, is so impressed by David's leadership and my quick obedience. His wife nods with a shine in her eyes and says she hopes she can become as compliant and submissive as I am. I feel a confusing mix of embarrassment and pride and push the exchange out of my mind.

There's a family from our church with whom we've become quite close. The husband is a police officer and David decides that he's finally found his calling. We've spent our entire marriage discussing his desire for countless occupations other than the one he has, but this one sticks with him for months. I have to put my foot down. I see my friend living the life of a police officer's wife with her four children, and with three of my own, I'm not starting at the bottom of that heap with night shifts and holiday and weekend hours.

There's another, unspoken reason I'm so dismayed by the idea of David as a cop: he's easily angered, incredibly sensitive and defensive, and he's tightly wound, jumpy. These attributes can come in handy, but aren't the safest combination for an officer of the law.

On a walk, we see a toddler playing at the ground floor living room window, pushing on the screen. Before I even have time to realize what's happening, the toddler is falling and David has left my side on the sidewalk, miraculously catching the child mid-air. His hyperawareness is certainly a check in the positive column when it comes to protecting and serving our community, but things escalate quickly one night when, while we're fast asleep, the waterproof CD player I bought him for his birthday falls from the shower wall with a startling crash. Before I'm even fully awake, David is wild-eyed in the living room with a bat. I have to explain to him what happened, speaking slowly to calm him down. These attributes are what David uses to assure me how good he would be as a civil servant, but there is a growing, nameless fear inside of me. I know police work will sharpen my fear and heighten David's growing issues. His sales career has morphed into an analyst position, and the salary is meager, but he has a secure job there. Maybe he's just bored.

He dives deeper into his spiritual studies and begins seeing entities in our home, spending hours praying them away. Once, I drive the girls alone to visit my mom and by the time we arrive eight hours later, Allana is grabbing her ear and screaming in pain. Without any indication from me that something is wrong, David calls and asks if Allana has pain coming from her left ear. It is, in fact, her left ear. He says he saw a dark presence beside her as he was praying, but not to worry, it's going to be gone in an hour or two. Within the next few hours, her pain subsides. It's not that I don't believe him; I have no problem believing that dark entities exist. It's just that I don't see them myself, so I'm not frightened by their potential. David's dramatic fervor makes me much more uncomfortable than any demon but I take it all in stride. Everything is to be taken seriously when eternity is on the line.

Mary lives in Boise now, only about 30 minutes away. She is not walking a righteous path, so we have her for dinner and *tsk* in dismay when she leaves. One night she goes to say goodnight to the girls and I walk in to see four year old Allana holding Mary's face in her hands.

"When you want to walk up and see that boy, don't go Mary. Make good choices!"

Mary is visibly shaken by the exchange and I know she needs to be folded into the flock, sheltered by the right choices like going to church, but I don't know how to keep her safe if she won't choose it for herself.

In 2005, the opportunity to keep her safe arrives suddenly, in the form of a change so big and impossible it feels like an adventure. We're moving. We're finally getting out of Idaho. Still working for Walgreens, David has been offered a new job in Wisconsin and decides to take it because there is a church nearby that promises the possibility of pastoral training. It's not a CREC church, but they read all the right books, including Doug's, and the pastor there preaches brilliantly and straight from the word of God.

I tell Mary she must come. I tell my mom that Mary is coming with us, that we will protect her. I am lit up with the frenzy of doing something, in taking action.

In very short order, everything is arranged. He goes to visit Wisconsin and feels the presence of the Lord. He knows now that being a pastor is all he's ever wanted. He buys us a house. I didn't see it beforehand but I don't care. I need this catapult of fiery action; burning down my life and starting over feels right. I can fit into my skinniest jeans again, a sure sign I'm heading in the right direction. I even have to buy new ones as I run around making sure all the pieces are in place. We say goodbye to our friends and family. We pack our lives into a semi which will be driven across the country to our new home, David drives our car the almost 2,000 miles, and the rest of us fly to meet him at our new home in Kenosha, WI.

I have been practicing my best Proverbs 31 woman routine and it pays off in my new home and community. Every morning I don my invisible garment of galvanized steel. I am an unstoppable force. The house is not what I thought it would be, but it has good qualities and I'm determined to make it right while accounting for every penny. The rabbit wallpaper in the kitchen comes off, as does the fake wood paneling in the enclosed porch. The panels in the basement and the loft bedrooms get coat after coat of paint. I splurge on a professional carpet cleaner in the bedrooms and shine the wood floors to a glossy mirror. As always, David's energy and good will is whipped into action anytime I'm spending myself on our home, children or him, and he joins in with gusto and unstoppable energy. We have people for dinner weekly. I prepare to homeschool the girls. I have countless talks with Mary while she helps me paint, and encourage her as she finds a new life for herself living in our basement.

My guilty pleasure is watching the show *Sister Wives* while I fold laundry. I watch it with an intense jealousy for having duties, both practical and sexual, divvied out. I fantasize about being able to have that kind of help and support. After every episode I take a deep breath to push my wicked thoughts away, look at my stacks of folded laundry, and keep moving.

In the midst of this transition, we dive headlong into our new church community. It's larger than what we're used to, and everyone is excited to welcome us. David tells anyone who will listen that his new job was merely the catalyst to get us across the country, that we have come for the biblical fellowship, for the training, for the growth.

We join a care group. Each group has ten or so members that meet weekly for Bible study and prayer, gathering often for meals and holidays. All care groups have a couple as their leaders, chosen for their godliness and wisdom.

The care group leaders also meet weekly to pray for one another as they lead their flock within the flock. We rise quickly in the ranks to gain leader status of our care group.

We join the Exploring Christianity ministry that meets weekly to answer any questions people have about the faith. It's a robust and thriving machine of an organization. The participating women of the church are all given the same recipe for a main dish, a salad, and a dessert, and we deliver our portions within a certain window of time to feed everyone a delicious, hot, free meal. One of the six pastors then gives a relatable, humorous talk on why it's so difficult (but necessary) to be a Christian, and everyone gathers into small groups to reflect upon the pastor's words. The theme of this entire church has been coined by the head pastor: "live for the line, not the dot." Our lives are merely a dot, a tiny space in time. But because we have souls, we will live on in eternity, separate from our bodies. Eternity is the infinite line and we spend the dot preparing for the line. Don't stop. Keep working. Keep striving. Do this all with joy because eternity is only a dot away.

Every day is centered around living for the line. To fill our tank, we get up early and read our Bibles. As a Christian woman, my home and children are the priority. I've been practicing this for years and run my household efficiently: three homemade meals a day, laundry done, home clean, children washed and well behaved, I even exercise via VHS tape or CD every afternoon while they nap to keep my body attractive. At our new church it's not a sin for the women to work outside the home or send their children to public school, but for the first time in my life I am one of the popular girls, clearly modeling how to do things right. This doesn't go to my head, frankly I'm too tired and busy to pay it much mind, but it does feel like a relief to be on the winning side for once. I think I've finally got the good Christian girl thing down for real this time.

This goes on for years. This mad, whirling, vortex of *doing*. Besides leading our in-home care group, I join the women's ministry team, we're both on the welcoming team, and we run a group at Exploring Christianity. Myself and a pastor's wife start a homeschooling co-op and call it Grace Academy. We feature the classical education curriculum from Canon Press, started by

Doug Wilson. It quickly grows and I take on the English class of 16 and the drama department of 40. I write a play based on *Pilgrim's Progress* and direct the production.

A group of moms takes a road trip to Nashville to the Classical Education Homeschooling conference. Along the way, I tell them the story of Wes Callihan, of Logos School, of Doug Wilson. I phrase it from the lens of forgiveness. I don't leave room for sympathy because I am already healed.

Still, when I come face to face with Doug Wilson himself in the crowded hallway on the second day of the conference, my body freezes for the first time in many years. He greets me and shakes my hand warmly.

"Jade, how are you?" he says.

I immediately start sobbing, loud and ugly, my body heaving. I am shocked and embarrassed by my outburst. Why is my body betraying me?

"God is bigger than all of it, isn't he?" I cry through my tears. "He's so good."

Doug nods sagely, a gentle smile on his face. Someone hands me a tissue. I find solace in a bathroom stall until I stop shaking. I reframe the message my body sent me: I know now how to contain all of it. My identity is in Christ. He is the engine pulling my faith along, my feelings are nothing more than a little caboose. I will draw upon facts to inform me of my feelings as I have been taught. I draw a cleansing breath and rejoin the conference, once again a composed Christian woman.

Back at home in the privacy of our bedroom, I am still using spermicide foam religiously. I hide when I get dressed for bed because if David sees a sliver of my body, he will want to have sex. We argue about it and finally create a calendar of days, at least two per week, where I consent to having sex with him. Martin Luther, father of Protestantism in the 16th century, wrote a lot about sex and said twice a week was enough to keep the devil at bay. The Bible clearly states that a wife doesn't have authority over her own body, nor does the husband. I do my duty in this as in everything else.

One morning the coffee doesn't smell good and I know in an instant that I'm pregnant. I cry when the pregnancy test is positive, beating my hand on the bathtub and wailing. Mary is dismayed for me. I am flooded with the knowledge that I absolutely do not want another baby. My quiver is too full. I am in a constant state of overwhelm. I miscarry, and David cries out to God and cannot be comforted. I tap into an emotion that postures like sadness but feels like relief, and write a beautiful poem about giving our little baby to God for safekeeping.

Meanwhile, Mary finds a husband in the church. They court, not date, the distinction is important. We plan the wedding. I arrange to have friends from Idaho come and sing, and prepare my house for family to come and stay. I create a document of the daily plan and the menu. I leave a copy with a chocolate on everyone's pillow. The wedding is simple but beautiful and Mary is safely tucked within the folds of our community. I have done my duty.

David is becoming increasingly more difficult to manage. I spend hours, sometimes daily, keeping him at bay. If he's not trying to control the children, he's complaining bitterly about how he isn't given the respect he deserves. I'm alarmed by his ability to be politician-nice one minute and bitter and mean the second he can't be seen or heard by anyone but me. He aims his vitriol at another pastor in the church, who he calls his best friend, at my sister and her husband, and our children, especially Allana who is the most like me. My little sister Kallie comes to live with us for a summer. She's reminiscent of me in my younger days, in active rebellion of all things holy, and David's disdain for her is palpable. Within months he demands she leave our house.

My brother comes to visit and brings with him a nasty cut on his arm from summer camp. It turns into cellulitis within days and our doctor, also an elder in our church, performs an emergency procedure. A week after Brian returns home I think I have a zit on my chin, but soon realize it's a spider bite. Over the course of one weekend my jaw swells so badly it's hard to open my mouth. There's a growing alarm in my body that something is very wrong. David is annoyed by my insistence and tells me to stop being dramatic. I drive myself to the ER early Sunday morning and am sent home with an antibiotic script and told to get a Benzoyl wash for my runaway zit. Still, I am increasingly aware something is amiss, this is far more than a runaway zit. I don't take my temperature but know I have a fever and, much to David's chagrin, call our doctor again later that afternoon. He comes to our front door, takes one look at me, asks for the name of the doctor that sent me home from the ER, and tells me to go back. Within an hour I'm in emergency surgery. The bite has evolved into cellulitis and gone septic, abscessed in two places. Our doctor makes sure I have the best plastic surgeon around to handle the cut with minimal scarring. I live, thanks to four different antibiotics and my gut instinct, but mostly thanks to the church. We take care of one another. We are family.

Cracks and tears are forming in the seams of my galvanized garment. It's showing its wear and tear. My health remains poor. My anemia is intense, brought on by bleeding so heavy I have to stay near a bathroom for days during my cycle. I drop lime-sized clots regularly now. The only iron pills I can stomach cost $80 a month, which we don't have to spare. We keep close tabs on our money out of necessity, creating an envelope of cash for every line item in our budget. I'm constantly maneuvering to make it work, such as changing the menu to find economical alternatives, skipping a haircut or three, or guiding the girls towards less expensive weekly activities.

In addition, I have chronic constipation that doesn't respond well to over the counter laxatives. I am forgetting things more than ever, often finding my keys in my hand even as I race around the house in a panic looking for them. I leave my wallet at one store or another at least once a week.

I am failing at mothering. My confident mask is slipping. The pressure of both raising and teaching my girls wears me thin. I am scary and mean when I feel overwhelmed. Learning how to read is supposed to be fun, but it isn't when I'm at the helm. I see the fear on my babies' faces and I feel sad, but I shove the sadness down and whip them into shape. The state of their soul is largely dependent on my doing everything correctly.

Sometimes I have to say horrible things to myself to force my body out of bed and into action. I'm so tired but I can't stop for a minute or everything will fall apart. Sophia finally breaks me. I don't spare her the rod but she doesn't care. From infancy, she has been my defiant child. She will not let me subdue her and one day, when she's four years old, I find myself holding her on the floor of my bedroom, crying with her because I don't know how to do it anymore. I don't know how to be a godly woman. There's a break, a surrender in my soul. I am deeply cognizant that something has to change in my life. What, I'm not sure, but I allow my body the admission that I'm not okay.

But then a miracle happens. David has been actively praying and waiting for two things: to have a son, and to be a pastor. He talks about it daily. This time when the coffee smells bad I don't wish it away. I don't want another baby, but I do want peace and, as usual, my weakness when pregnant, any neediness in general, turns David pliant and caring. I know in my soul it's a boy and tell him so. For what must be the millionth time, I talk to him about sending the girls to school and he finally relents. I won't be able to get a job as I wanted, but I content myself with releasing the burden of educating my children single-handedly and dive into the deep end of motherhood yet again.

The pattern repeats. When I'm pregnant or have a small baby or toddler, all I can do is keep my head above water with no time to worry about how I feel. Additionally, I stop bleeding during pregnancy which allows me to shore up on iron. My body functions beautifully when I'm pregnant and nursing, so I give in to the wonder of my tiny baby boy. There are some rather serious interruptions: part of the placenta is left in my body and I fall very ill. Jack, at a mere three days old, barks out a strange cough and starts throwing up all his milk in a geyser-like manner that I intuitively know is not normal. Still, I manage to get the girls to school in the mornings and have hours alone to take care of the baby, clean the house, and start dinner. I bake after school treats for the girls and find my happiness again.

Not long after Jack arrives, David gets his second wish. There's a vacancy on the pastoral team and David knows in his soul the job is his. He has a wife busy at home with a quiver full of children, the all-important addition of a son, and now he will finally be at peace with the job he was meant to do. I can do nothing but be swept up by the current of his dream to serve. I am interviewed by the rest of the pastoral team and the elders in the church. They ask me if David meets the biblical qualifications to lead the flock. They go through them one by one, pausing, looking at me significantly to get my answer. I am presence and composure all over again. Not violent? Not quarrelsome? Managing his household well? Self controlled? There are at least ten. David fails many categories but my mind won't let me comprehend it in the moment; he WILL be all of these things once he finally has the job he was meant to do in this lifetime, so I'm not exactly lying as I sing his praises.

There's also the small but significant matter of me, myself, and I. I thought I was doing so well in this specific church community, but there is a concern, voiced by another of the pastor's wives, that I am not modest enough. A meeting is held to discuss the problem at hand. David is asked to speak to me about toning it down. I look in my closet, searching for problematic garments. It must be the hot pink Calvin Klein dress I got off the clearance rack at Marshall's. David says I shouldn't worry about it. He's proud to have such a sexy wife, no wonder everyone is jealous.

He gets the position and we are launched into a new world, the upper echelon of the six pastors and their wives and families, leading the church with harmony, joy, and hard work, leading by example.

I'm exhausted by the constant harping on my bright and shiny, a shine that's becoming dimmer with every passing year of Jack's sickness. We spend a lot of time assuming he has allergies. My search for the right food for myself while nursing, and then later for him, takes me on a journey to heal many of my own body's symptoms, for which I can only be grateful.

A well-known allergist fears Jack has cystic fibrosis and sends us to the children's hospital for a battery of horrific tests. They all come back negative. During a surgery to remove Jack's adenoids, which are blocking 90% of his airway, he's finally diagnosed by his ENT with subglottic stenosis. Jack has been cycling through croup and every lung infection known to man since birth. His daily, constant cough sounds like a child dying from pneumonia and I play the part of the insensitive mother who has him out in public. I am used to every head in the grocery store and library swiveling towards me, faces stricken with terror and accusation. The catch in his airway causes him to throw up unexpectedly several times a day, often in public. The long, incessant Wisconsin winters are the worst for his condition, the humid summers not much better. He needs a hot, dry climate, one like southern Idaho, but our lives are here.

Despite our son's sickliness, managing David has become my main priority. The stress of pastoring is proving to be more than he bargained for. Besides his weekly duties, he has a lot of public speaking, which is simply not his forte, and yet he has to do it constantly between prayers, stating announcements, and giving updates to our congregation of over 1,000 over two sermons. He fears failure and it seems to me that every Sunday feels like a failure to him. I spend countless hours talking him down from the ledge or out of the abyss.

I try to stand between him and the girls as much as possible. As they get older he regards their behavior suspiciously, reminding me of his mother. Once during a visit, eight year old Allana lifted her shirt to wipe her mouth and she slapped Allana's hands, shouting that only a hussy shows her midriff. David is constantly hissing at me about our girls' behavior, fearing the worst. Being alone with him is a chore that's becoming more and more of a heavy burden.

His consistent negativity takes on a new twist when he catches Audrey holding hands with a boy in 8th grade. The way he treats her is as if she's whored herself out. He puts much of the blame on me because I have offered Audrey too much freedom with her friends. The honest truth is Audrey and her small group of friends have offered me solace, a time and place to relax. I invite them over because they make me laugh and love my cinnamon toast. For Audrey's birthday, I drive her and her friends to Devil's Lake for the day and the easy camaraderie I feel with them is a warning to me. I am aware that something is very wrong if I feel more comfortable and prefer the company of 12 and 13 year olds to anyone else I know.

David's favorite strategy is to start a fight when we're driving because I can't leave. The calmer I am the angrier he gets. One night I can't take it anymore and I scream at him, "Jesus can SEE and HEAR you right now!" and, as he's rolling the car to a stop, I open the door and run into the rain, sobbing and determined to get away. Just as when we were first married, as soon as I mirror him by becoming frenzied or passionate, he always becomes more passive.

One sunny afternoon at home, the girls are outside playing with Jack when David starts to pick a fight. I refuse to respond to his nonsense this time and instead start laughing at his ludicrous behavior. He's becoming more and more ridiculous to me. Within seconds he has me on my back, his fist aimed at my face.

"Go ahead," I say, my voice like steel. I stare at him, unblinking. "Go ahead and hit me."

We hear the girls bringing Jack in for his nap and quickly rearrange our positions. I hurry into the bathroom to regain my composure and look into the mirror. What I see there is a woman, now in her late 30s, with no career, no job, no college degree, and no money of her own. I have painted myself into a corner. I am trapped with no way out.

To the Outside Girl, with Love

Oh the power of your body to cast and create!

Congratulations, you are officially the master of blaming yourself.

It's a narrative you have invented; you are so powerful, and you don't want to be the victim, so you bring blame to yourself in a way that is convincing, logical, and believable to yourself and others.

Even when it doesn't fit, you make it fit.

Oh how you rationalize your feelings instead of just feeling them.

You beat yourself up to whip yourself into line, and your system has learned to detach in order to enable.

To keep yourself safe, you have fashioned a wall around your heart, made of material as hard as diamonds and clear as glass.

You stand behind it, pretending you are present in your world, appearing to be right there, but in reality you are alone.

Darling, this wall? It must be destroyed. You are too important.

My words have been harsh, I know, so let me brag on you for a moment.

You know how to make something out of nothing, and your something is magnificent.

It's stunning, it's beautiful.

It's a light for others when all seems dark.

You shine bright and flow, even if it's seeping through the cracks of the façade.

You cannot be contained.

Hold on, my dear.

The only way out is through.

V

Pluto Square Pluto

"The opposite of slut is not virtue, but voice." Lacy Crawford

9

The Quickening

I hate running, I hate it with a passion. David loves it. He has even decided to train for a marathon, so we purchase a gigantic mechanical contraption of a treadmill, put it in the basement, and he pounds away during the long Wisconsin winter. The incessant thud of his feet reverberates through the vents and makes me insane.

Ironically, the treadmill becomes my new best friend as well. I find that David can't complain if I take time for myself by mimicking him. I leave the sound of him, the children, and the ever-present needs of the household behind as I don my iPod headphones. For motivation I download a playlist for runners. This is an act of rebellion, especially for a pastor's wife. The Bible is very clear about being careful what you listen to, and warns that "out of the heart proceed all manners of evil."

In our home we listen to classical music. David listens to several Christian artists in the rock and rap genres, but I think they sound ridiculous. I love to cook to the trilling notes of Miles Davis or Coltrane. Sometimes we go really crazy and put in a CCR CD, but for the most part I've listened to no secular music since the late 90's and it's now 2012. I have a lot of catching up to do.

Is it the endorphins or the words that wake me up? I can't be sure, but when I run, I'm viscerally reminded of the youth government trip, the dorm room, the Def Leppard song, and I realize it's all happening again.

Like Rihanna's "Only Girl," I want to know what it's like when time and space have no meaning. I run and sweat to countless Black Eyed Peas songs. I too want to drown in something I can't get enough of; there's so much I haven't allowed myself to feel.

I listen intently as I move in the rhythm of the songs. The unending rubber track has become my sacred place. There are layers of lies I've told myself and I am shedding them, sweating them out: "no one actually feels that depth of passion" (false), "marriage is better if it's more about teamwork and less about love" (false), "your husband, children, and home are your only real concern" (false).

My body innately knows what living is supposed to feel like, it aches with the knowing, energy with no place to go. I am missing something I don't have. I'm unable to articulate it as I come up from the basement, glowing with sweat and lust. This feels like a secret, like my own personal genie in a bottle, waiting to grant me a wish.

I attempt to bring David along for the ride. I try to spice it up. A church member knocks on our door on a Saturday morning, Allana answers and, in her pure honesty, says her parents are in the shower. It's no secret what we're doing there. Another time we stop in the woods on the way to Exploring Christianity to have sex in the car. David is not shy; he crows about our active sex life and I join in with a smile, shaking my head.

Everyone is constantly commenting on our picture perfect family. My husband is the epitome of the Christian husband: he does dishes, cleans the house, and worships the ground I walk on. At church he's most often seen with our children in his arms, his hand protectively around my waist. I am a lucky, lucky woman. I try to feel the truth of the picture painted for me. I've been trying for 18 years.

My sweet baby brother gets married. He is a rising star in Doug Wilson's cohort and he and his bride marry young after a short courtship, both fresh out of Doug's newly-minted, but non-accredited, New Saint Andrew's college. Mary and I fly to Idaho for the celebration with my new, tiny niece, just the three of us.

As no one else in our family had to force him out of their lives, Jason is at the outdoor wedding with his fiancée who gives me a death glare. My body can no longer contain the lie that I did the right thing by cutting him out. I ask him to step aside with me and words immediately pour out, unchecked and unplanned. He speaks his words too, how I have hurt him beyond measure and he feels like he lost his family. We stand there, in the semi-dark, as long as we need to, tears and hugs flowing freely. When I come back to the reception my body feels lighter. I feel so good and instinctively I know I won't be able to stop the shedding. I'm reclaiming something, though still nameless, and it's picking up steam now.

As Jack nears age three and I learn to manage his symptoms, I am determined to find myself beyond the labels of wife and mother, but still I cling to the only structure I know, trying to contain my glow within the confines of my galvanized garment. We join the YMCA and I utilize the daily two free hours of childcare. I explain Jack's condition and his cough so they understand and let the other mothers know he's not infectious. I take every aerobics class known to man. I make friends with one of the teachers and learn to lift weights. I can do 20 plank-to-pike reps on the TRX straps. I pretend not to flirt with Max, a fireman who somehow finds his way to all the same classes I attend.

At home, I host epic dinner parties, choosing complicated, four course meals and do all the cooking myself. Games are included and, just like elementary school, I make them up. My favorite is a twist on charades: I cut up countless strips of paper, and in one bowl place handwritten situations like, "an airplane flight," "a visit to the salon," and "ordering food at a restaurant." Another pile is characters such as, "a police officer," "a two year old," or "a mob boss." I split everyone into groups and the winners are judged by how well they embody their character and riff off their other team members' characters. At first my guests are hesitant, but I insist and the scenes we play out leave us laughing until we cry and become all we can talk about at church for weeks after. When a respected airline captain has to order food at a restaurant as a two year old, and his svelte wife is playing a mob boss who's taking the order, the hilarity comes naturally.

We are close with our friends, both those in our care group and the other pastor's families. We share our lives together, cook together, and spend holidays together. There's a sweet couple from Arizona who we walk beside through pregnancy and a battle with leukemia when their daughter is but a toddler. Another longtime member struggling with her addict son has a pulmonary embolism in our living room during care group. I hold her on my lap on the floor as she clutches her chest, gasping for air, and we pray over her while we wait for the ambulance. Miraculously, she survives. I help care for a blind woman in our group and say goodbye to her on her deathbed when cancer finally takes her. My entire life is wrapped in and around these people.

Yet I have a growing feeling that David and I are separate entities. After almost 20 years of consciously and subconsciously considering myself as his wife above all else, there is a growing need for independence, for keeping myself busy enough to not have to deal with him. The tantrums, the menacing physical stances, the bitter complaints behind closed doors, the nasty words aimed with venom at our children, my sister and her husband, at the other pastors, have never stopped. I continue to tiptoe on the proverbial egg shells strewn all over the floor. There is nowhere safe to step.

The truth is, I've never truly felt completely safe or free being intimate with him. When we have sex I choose the top more and more and move until I cum, at which he complains that he feels like I'm using him. My body freezes when he comes in for a hug or a kiss; he's constantly trying to grab my nipples or slap my butt, and I hate it. My denial of his advances makes him angry, and he often lashes out, but I don't trust him. I can't say those words out loud in my head or my heart; the fact that I've never been completely comfortable around him is a secret buried so deep under the surface it's never seen the light of day.

I lobby to work outside the home again. It takes hours of conversation with David and assurances that I won't shirk my duties. Mary gets me the job; she's a commission only sales rep at a new up-and-coming chocolate company and they need a second. The chocolate is ethically sourced, bean to bar, with boutique worthy ingredients like orange peel, pink peppercorns, and candied ginger. It's a stellar team to work for. The owner, Jonathan, works full time in a well known tech company and is the brains of the business. His wife, Kate, is an interior designer and the organizer of operations extraordinaire. Jonathan's sister, also a Mary, is a graphic designer. They're smart, young, hip. They eat paleo, do resistance training, and take their business seriously. Mary and I are proud to work for them.

Beautifully packaged samples are sent to specific locations around the country. My job is simple: call and make sure I'm talking to the decision maker before I pitch an order based on the sample they received. Immediately I excel. It's like a fun game, getting the right person on the phone and, if they haven't already indulged, inviting them to find our package and try the chocolate sample right there and then on the phone. On the phone, my name sounds like I'm saying "Katie" and it's constantly confusing my clients, so I change the pronunciation of my name from Jade-y to Jade. I begin to sign my emails, "All the Best, Jade." It feels right, another layer of shedding.

I am shining again and my light is brighter than it's ever been. I am in charge of my domain, I'm giving David less of my energy and ignoring his bitter retorts, my children are safe, and I have time to thrive in my own body and mind. This sliver of space I've carved out for myself, using my natural skill set to make my own money, however little, is like the freshly whipped cream I make for my pumpkin pie - almost as good as the pie itself.

I fall into a pleasant rhythm of both chatting via messenger and talking to Jonathan on the phone after I've taken the girls to school and before I go to the Y. Our conversations become more and more personal as we realize we can make one another laugh in sheer, honest delight. His analytical intelligence accompanies a dry sense of humor and I love surprising him with what I'll say next.

"What are you doing now?" he asks one morning. Neither of us want to hang up.

"Getting ready to go to the Y, same as every morning." I respond. He knows this already, though.

"Mmmhmm...and what's your favorite part of your routine?"

"Stretching at the end. I'm lifting today. I have my own little brand of yoga meets pilates, but I really just move my body any way that feels yummy."

Jonathan laughs, instantaneous and husky.

"I've never heard anyone mix up their five senses so indiscriminately."

"I've never been one to color inside the lines," I say. "I mean, I've tried, but I'm really bad at it."

"It seems to me you're very good at it. Look at your life. Lots of boxes. You're staying in the lines beautifully."

I need to change the subject.

"Speaking of stretching, the other morning this sweet old woman just stared at me from her recumbent bike while I was stretching. She just stared and smiled as she pedaled away, and I smiled back and kept going. Afterward she gestured at me to come closer and told me I looked just like a cat stretching after a sunbath."

"I've never seen you in person, but I can imagine that's a fairly accurate description."

"Mmmm, maybe! Being sun drunk is definitely one of my favorite things."

"There you go again. Hmmmm...I think I'll call you Catniss. And Jade," he pauses. "We definitely need to meet."

I can't admit to the thrill this brings me, but as coworkers, it seems innocent enough to make it happen. If the entire team meets in the middle, we all travel an hour round trip, and so begins a series of team meetings, their frequency growing at the same pace as Jonathan and my fascination with one another. In fact, fascination is too weak of a word to describe the thrumming electricity. We start to find marketing opportunities at high end grocery stores and boutiques near Chicago, both to grow the business and as an excuse to connect. Jonathan works downtown and I make myself available, so it's usually just the two of us. I am a hot air balloon, capable of rising 11 stories in height but only recently unfurled. When I'm in physical proximity to Jonathan it's another ignition, another firing of the blast valve, and liftoff becomes inevitable; there are not enough tethers in the world to keep me from launching.

Jonathan is not particularly handsome, not in a traditional sense. He's several years younger than me, with a shock of dark hair, piercing, light brown eyes, and slim, lean muscles. On days when we're not together, he sends me his poetry. It's very, very good. Delicious, succulent even. He's also an accomplished pianist and he takes it up again. He writes music at a prolific pace, but won't play me his pieces, not yet. I am his muse. I know this in my bones and this time I'm ready to guide, to personify, to embody.

The first time we kiss, it's a stolen moment away from the shop. We've gone to look at his old keyboard I'm purchasing for Sophia, and he plays his new piece that he wrote for me. It's breathtakingly beautiful. I know an artist when I see one, or in this case, hear one. It's a feeling that lights me up and I have to taste it, taste him. He tastes like the brine of the ocean, salt on my tongue, with the scent of air so sweet and warm you could breathe it in forever.

I am completely cognizant of what I'm doing. My sin is unforgivable. My life will never be the same, but it is already ruined as it is. Even before the kiss I had taken a torch and set fire to the forest that was my life. I know this and it can't stop me. I am no longer able to beat, cajole, shame, or guilt myself into my garment each morning. There are too many ripped seams, too many holes to manage; even galvanized iron breaks down under certain conditions. I am left naked and bare and it feels like a promise.

I am chosen to go to Madison for a marketing event. This will require overnight travel. David is not pleased but I give him no choice in the matter. Jonathan tells Kate he is on a work trip for his day job, but of course plans to join me. He books one hotel room in the mansion hill historic district, and we barely make it through the event.

As we sit at the table, smiling at customers, fielding their questions, I feel his fingers moving up my leg and under my skirt. He knows I don't wear panties, he is one of the few people who knows and loves the story of why I haven't worn underwear of any sort since I was 18. I am dripping with a hot, pulsing need. I can't breathe. We get up, blind with lust and want, and somehow make it to the hotel. The thigh-high socks I've chosen specifically for him stay on, as does my short plaid skirt, and my legs are in the air. He drinks me in, like he's been dying of thirst, and I am off, launched into another stratosphere. I come and go in waves. I have every orgasm possible; God, it's good to be a woman. We have stamina. We make love, we fuck, we invade every square inch of the suite until we're puddles on the floor.

Eventually, we notice it's gotten dark and we dissolve into hysterics when we realize we've been at it for over three hours. We go out into the balmy summer night and eat and drink and say filthy things in one another's ears. We come back to the room and slowly, sweetly savor one another over and over, wincing through our giggles as we realize everything is sore.

For months we stay at it like this. Once, he is out for a delivery and brings his van close to where I live. All we have time for is to meet quickly in a parking lot, and we have sex inside the van, in broad daylight, with the windows and doors closed to shield us from the basketball players a few yards away. When we emerge over an hour later, we have utilized all the space in the back and are dripping with sweat and completely dehydrated. We're amazed by ourselves. Who does this? We do, apparently.

We have holidays together with our spouses and entwine our legs under the table. His parents' house is in the middle of our respective towns so we often meet there when they're not home, like we're teenagers experiencing freedom for the first time. Our moments are stolen, precious, and we fill every hour we have locked in a need so fierce that the only way to communicate it, satiate it, is with our bodies.

These months feel like some sort of delayed becoming, like I'm taking back my right to evolve and cramming it in as fast as possible, knowing it can't last. All of my senses are clear and heightened these days. I've learned the importance of smell. Everything about him smells incredible to me; his natural scent is an aphrodisiac. When it comes to David, I wash the sheets and pillowcases as much as possible and ask him to shower before we have sex, though sex has become almost impossible with David. I cry in the dark and feel like I'm cheating on Jonathan. The lies and the sneaking are wearing me down. I need to be alone with Jonathan more and more. I need to escape my current life, which has begun to choke me with the impossibility of continuing on and pretending I'm all the things I've been painted to be. I'm simply not her anymore.

I beg Jonathan for another "work trip" and he acquiesces but does so hesitantly. His logic and reason are returning and Kate is getting suspicious.

Our bliss, the food, the orgasms, are just as intense on a trip to Ann Arbor, but he is interrupted constantly by calls from Kate, which I often listen in on from the car or from bed. After one agonizing call I recognize the similarities in Kate and David: for one thing, they both certainly love to complain about people behind their back. More than that, I've lived with David for 20 years and I have an inner knowing that their personalities would mesh.

"Kate and David would make a great couple," I quip.

Jonathan looks surprised and then we both start laughing. Wouldn't that be convenient though?

I don't know it at the time, but the trip to Ann Arbor that October is the last we will ever take together. On this trip, I can't bear to have him pull out of me, and anyway, we've had sex so often with this supposedly ineffective method that nothing could possibly happen, right? I take the Plan B pill when we get back, but my body betrays me. Out of all the times I've gotten pregnant, four out of five times have been in October, three resulting in births and one in a miscarriage. This makes five out of six.

We meet at his parents' house on a perfect sunny day in early November, and I show him the Clearblue Easy test strip. I've caught it very early, I'm probably no more than four weeks along. Jonathan is stunned. We cycle through wonder that we've created a life, to talking about how we could possibly make it work, to a bone deep recognition that this is not a possible scenario. I imagine my life with an infant a hundred times, and each time my body tells me it's not a healthy choice. Jonathan confesses that he uses a powerful drug to keep him from going bald, one that can be passed through the sperm and causes almost certain birth defects. This solidifies the decision, but besides that, Jonathan has known since he was a teen that he wouldn't bring a child into the world. Kate has been on birth control since they've been married, something they've fought about for years and worked hard on to reach a place of peace. I toss my head, angry and affronted. What do I care what he and Kate have decided? This is about us. We call and make an appointment at a clinic in Chicago.

Two days later, I pick him up and we drive to the clinic. He pays at the front desk and we're escorted into a sterile, unwelcoming room. This is fine with me. This process deserves only ugliness. There is nothing warm and beautiful about this decision but, oddly enough, I am fully present and in my body. I'm not eager to do this, but I know I must. There are a million reasons I must.

Though I've spent decades proclaiming the ultimate evil of abortion, I feel no need to explain my decision. I have already burned down my life and this is simply part of the carnage. They ask me if I want Jonathan to come back with me, seeming surprised when I say yes, and even more confused when we both get weepy as they confirm the heartbeat. I don't know why the tears come; I'm not weeping with sorrow for what has to be done, or even what could have been, that's not for me to know. Still, I hate that I'm in this place, on this table, and my body knows. I feel a deep sorrow for the countless women I have judged that found themselves in a similar predicament, or much worse; this helps me stay present. I am resolute in my knowledge that I cannot house this possible life, there's simply no room. I'm only five weeks along so they give me a pill. I swallow it and we drive away to find a place to have sex in the car before I take him home. That's that.

They told me I would bleed a lot and, like so many other doctors, tested my blood to find it lacking in the iron department, impressing upon me the need to be careful. I bleed on and off throughout November and begin to suffer through the holidays. I lock myself in the bedroom and wrap presents for hours, weeping with the impossibility of my double life.

The only high points are when I can leave the house to shuttle my girls to their various practices, rehearsals, and school events. Otherwise, I am completely inconsolable if I can't reach Jonathan at all times. He's purchased me an iPhone, I've only had a flip phone up until this point, and I use it to try and stalk him. He gets wise to my antics and puts his phone on airplane mode, leaves me on read, takes Kate away on a birthday trip, goes to movies and weekly date nights with her, and I am suddenly a raging maniac. I cannot play nice with David and I don't understand Jonathan.

To console me, Jonathan tells me that he made reservations months before to a Michelin star rated restaurant in Chicago for a post Christmas celebration. It's exclusive, impossible to find, a speakeasy type location off an alleyway, and it will be a once in a lifetime meal. Of course, he explains, he couldn't justify taking just me but has invited the whole team: Kate, both Marys, another new sales rep Mary has found, and me. I buy a sexy black cocktail dress and, despite the blizzard outside, keep my legs bare and don my highest heeled shoes for the trek to Chicago. David follows me around as I get ready. He's confused, dismayed, he tries to fight with me, yells that he won't allow me to leave, that whatever is going on must stop. I agree.

I turn to look him dead in the eyes and say coldly, "I'm leaving right now. I'll be home late. Tomorrow I will tell you exactly what's going on."

I mean those words. I am finished with this game and tired of being a liar. Tonight will be perfect and tomorrow I will start my new life.

The restaurant is fire and ice, with flames rising from one dish, and cold slabs and crushed ice for the next work of art. Jonathan crows to the team about our success and we make toasts and beam shiny smiles into the candlelight. I'm mostly oblivious to anything but Jonathan's hand on my naked thigh, caressing me in the semi darkness.

We're finishing the second course and my head is turned away from Jonathan and Kate as I have a conversation with my sister. I hear a muffled exclamation and turn my head just in time to see Kate stand up abruptly, grab her handbag, and leave the room. The waiters come with the next round and say they'll wait for her to return from the bathroom, but Jonathan, his face drained of all color, urges them to serve the rest of us. We ooh and ahh as they pour the sauces, light their flames, and finally retreat. Jonathan then stands and leaves the table without a word.

I am woozy with wine and food, and the underlying knowledge that something portentous is happening. It was bound to. Everything that had gone on between us was leading up to this moment. Everyone else at the table is growing uneasy too, so a few minutes later I stand up and announce that I'll check on Jonathan. Both sister-Marys look at me sharply, but I calmly place my napkin on my chair, walk down the velvety quiet hall to find the men's restroom and enter, balanced precariously on a razor's edge between panic and excitement.

I see Jonathan leaning heavily on the counter, clearly in the midst of a panic attack. I navigate him out of the restroom and we find a secluded corner to talk.

"She's left," Jonathan whispers raggedly. "Kate's left and I have no idea where she went. I still have the keys and she didn't bring shoes for this weather."

I gaze at him, vaguely irritated. Why is this all about Kate right now?

"And?" I demand, insensitive to anyone's plight but my own at this point.

"She was picking up her napkin off the floor and saw my hand up your skirt. I thought she went to the bathroom but the coat check says she took her coat and left. Oh my God." He can barely breathe, all his team captain bravado has been swallowed by this catastrophic turn of events.

"It was going to happen eventually," I say, crisply.

I am calm under pressure, even when it comes to an actual catastrophe, like the time David and I were in a seven-car pileup on black ice. I called the insurance company while the EMTs took David's blood pressure because he was so panicked. I can be stoic; I know what needs to be done.

"We knew this was going to happen, now it has, and we will deal with it. This will get the ball rolling so we can be together."

Jonathan nods weakly but we agree to go back to the table, finish the other courses, and keep the conversation going as if nothing has happened. Jonathan explains to the others that Kate suddenly fell ill and she had to leave. From the looks on their faces, everyone knows this isn't true but we soldier on and cut dessert short.

After dinner, Jonathan asks his sister to pull up the car, giving him a few moments to sit in the passenger seat of mine. We exchange passionate kisses and discuss driving away together to spend the night at a hotel, leaving everything to be dealt with tomorrow, but Jonathan says he has to make sure Kate is alright, that she's safe. He tells me that his sister already knows about us; she saw us kissing once outside the chocolate shop. She's disgusted with him, but has had her own shit to deal with. Kate, on the other hand, is clearly devastated and Jonathan is panicked as he recognizes that he has put their business on the line just as they're becoming successful. I hush him, telling him for the hundredth time that everything will work out. He can have me, and he can have his business. What's meant to be will be.

I drive away in personal elation that all is going to be in the open. 10 minutes into my drive home my phone vibrates. It's my sister. Her voice is incredulous, accusing, confused, and I can't make out what she's saying, but slowly realize her car was behind mine and her headlights have caught our silhouettes. She's seen us kissing. Finally I hear a clear sentence cut through my haze.

"Do you want to tell me what's going on?!"

10

I Will Not Go Gently Into That Good Night

Time has no meaning now. I'm lost in an amorphous cloud. I am the cloud, floating, changing shapes with no explanation. I've never been one of these women, the kind to waste away from unrequited love, yet here I am. A tiny, ragged corner of my mind recognizes with wonder that I've swallowed the whole novel trope hook, line, and sinker. I am *Great Expectations, Anna Karenina, Remains of the Day,* and *Sense and Sensibility,* all rolled into one ball of despair. I am the antagonist, not the heroine. I am no *Tess of the D'Urbervilles,* a demure maiden, suffering because I've been taken advantage of by a scoundrel. I am nothing more than the prophecy laid out for me since age 14.

Buried in my covers for the fourth day in a row, unable to choke down food, surviving on just a few sips of water, I'm not thinking of my countless hours spent lost in those books, adrift in the romantic landscape of languishing lovers. I'm in the thick of it now and it is unmeasurable. It is a crushing weight. My children creep in to touch the sheets. They whisper, "Mama? Mom, are you okay?" I am not. I am not okay. I have tried to be a pure woman for so long, living for God first, and doing so for them. I glimpsed freedom and I fled towards it, but now I feel even my children are lost to me.

It all started according to plan. David was waiting up for me when I got home the night of Kate's discovery. He demanded a reckoning, spat threats, took menacing physical postures, even tried to force sex, but I was more resolute than ever before in my life. I was completely unphased. I had traded my ragged garment for a personal bubble of freedom. I had poured the final can of kerosene on the remaining fragments of my life, and told him he would wait until the morning, he would not wake the children, he would hear the truth on my terms.

I told him everything the next morning as I promised I would, baldly in places and bullet points in others. He immediately called the head pastor and demanded I get in the car. To keep the children from being further exposed, I acquiesced. At the church, trapped in a vast conference room with David and the pastor, I told the story again, woodenly and straight to the point. The details were a waste of time to me, I was already emotionally detached, gone to be with Jonathan. We had messaged one another the night before and both agreed to tell our respective spouses that we were leaving them for one another and then meet up later. I just wanted to get through this part and straight into his arms.

The pastor wept. David sobbed. I could not be shaken. They begged me to repent and ask for forgiveness. I stood up and started to walk out of the room. David intercepted me and opened his arms wide, tears streaming down his face.

"I forgive you! I forgive you!" he cried.

I pushed his arms away.

"You will never forgive me for doing this. Nor should you," I said, soundly.

This I knew without a doubt. Our entire marriage I had received the litany of pain and trauma his father's affairs had caused him. It was the lowest of lows, the number one sin in his mind. Fine. Good. I didn't want his drummed up forgiveness at that moment. I wanted him to let me go, but it was clear that wasn't going to happen. For the rest of the intervention, I simply sat, stone-like, floating above my body once again, and waiting for it to be over.

As soon as we pulled into the driveway I took the keys from David and told him I was leaving. I sent a text to Jonathan that my hard part was over and that I was on my way to the shop, a full hour away. My tiny Honda Civic had put in countless miles driving to meet him.

It was snowing again. December and January had been the bleakest winter months I'd experienced in my 10 years living in Wisconsin. It seemed poetic, blankets of white covering the burned forest floor of my life thus far, creating blank space for everything to rest.

And there he was, the shop almost completely dark, his face and body in the shadows. I ran towards him, full of giddy hope and ready for anything, ready for anything except the words that came out of his mouth. They were impossible words that took me over an hour to comprehend. He held my fists in his hands as I tried to beat his chest.

"Don't make this harder for me than it already is," he kept saying.

Harder for him?! I was incensed. I had left my God, my children, my community, the entirety of my belief structure for him, but when Kate opened her arms, begged him to come back and promised to forgive him, he gave in and admitted he had made a mistake. He said what we had done was wrong. His message was clear: he would never give up his life with Kate, or his business, for a good lay.

On the fifth day of my hibernation, I emerge from my cave of blankets and take a shower. Scrambled eggs are my first meal, coffee my first real beverage. While I've been down, my friends from the last 20 years, including my sister and mother, have been made aware of the "situation" and have been discussing it together. Collectively, they diagnose me with late onset bipolar disorder, and decide that I should (perhaps) be committed. My behavior is very serious, completely out of left field.

"She is clearly not in her right mind," they whisper.

I'm not. I have become a wooden doll, more Pinocchio than Pinocchio himself, but my stiff body stays upright as I navigate my personal bubble of freedom. I feel better in this space than anywhere else. In my head, "fuck" has become my favorite word. *I don't give a FUCK. And yes, I like to FUCK, but my literal inability to yield to the pressure of your call for my repentance is none of your FUCKING business.* I've never said fuck before out loud. How have I gone 38 years without saying FUCK?

The church is on a mission to bring me back into the fold. One of my friends, Karen, (I still have none outside the church) offers me her spare bedroom so I have a quiet space to think. Another friend, fairly new to the faith so still a believer in professional help, begs me to let her pay for any therapist of my choosing so I can get my thoughts in order. I accept their offers, not gracefully but resolutely.

During the day I stay with my children while David goes pastoring. I can't imagine what's happening at work every day with the shit storm I have created, but frankly I don't care. At home he is on a mission; he wakes me up when I'm sleeping to ask me if I'll come back to the marriage, leaves letters on my pillow, and hands me books about forgiveness and repair. None of his efforts penetrate my bubble. The utter relief I feel at no longer having to pacify him, try and convince him of my point of view, cajole him into good moods, or manage his hair-trigger temper makes it physically impossible to consider returning.

My girls are now 16, 14, and 11 and Jack is 4. They have questions. Their confusion and sorrow kill me, so I say little to nothing to them. They dance around me like sad fairies, trying to find me, unable to, and retreat to their corners of the house. I can't help them because in my wooden state, I no longer have a soul.

During the day, I take care of my children, I clean the house and make them food, I take them to school, and ferry them here and there. But as soon as David gets home, I leave and go to Karen's house and sleep like the dead. I make pleas to Jonathan via the secret email addresses we created, and finally receive a threat from Kate to stay away. He's given her the passwords to everything. He really isn't coming back.

I find a therapist, my first ever. I choose her in a bumbling, shot in the dark fashion, but after our first session I know without a doubt I like her. She asks the most brilliant questions, I talk, and she reframes, putting things into perspective.

"Oh darling. NO ONE is in favor of abortion… until they need one," she states with certainty.

She gives me the analogy of being on a raft in the middle of the ocean in a storm. I only have one oar but I have enough water and food to survive and know how to navigate by the stars. So, even though it feels like I won't make it, I can, and I will.

Every Sunday, David takes the kids to church and I hold my own service: Bon Iver's "Skinny Love" on repeat while I sob. How had I gone 38 years without choosing music I wanted to listen to?

I am called into the head pastor's office one day. I go because he called me personally and politely asked me if I would come. He said he had some questions he would like to ask me. Like my new therapist, he is very good at asking questions and I'm curious.

We have a meeting of the minds, he and I. He admits he had seen some red flags from David long ago. He peers kindly into my eyes and asks if there's more to the situation than meets the eye. Duh. He asks if I will repent, return to the fold, be honest about my marriage, and go about healing it in the right way.

"We're not asking you to return to the life you had," he says, somberly. "I agree with you; that life is gone. I'm begging you, before God, to repent of your sins and come back to the church so we can walk with you. All can be repaired and rebuilt. You're not alone."

But I am. I am alone on my raft in the middle of the ocean, facing my own storm, and I know I can find my way back myself. I must. I owe myself that much. I know how to navigate by the stars, in ways I never knew I could! My freedom bubble is much more comfortable than my galvanized garment, despite my wooden state. I'm taking back my right to change and grow. I say "fuck" now. I listen to Beyonce's "Drunk in Love" and swoon with a desire to taste life.

I don't bother to explain this to the pastor. His agenda is too narrow and I don't trust him. Instead, I lean forward in my seat and say, "I will not repent on your timeline. I don't even know what that word means anymore. But I'll give you this: when you interviewed me before David became a pastor and asked me those questions? I lied. I lied for him and that was wrong. Please forgive me." I stand up and I leave.

There's one last ditch collective effort to save me: I'm offered a week-long retreat in Milwaukee at the home of an older couple affiliated with the church. They want nothing more than to give me some space and time to think, away from the weight of David's persistent sorrow-rage and my children's very real need to be mothered. Members of the church will take care of the children and tend to David. I go, but I go with a secret. Just days before, my phone had dinged with a text from a number I had erased but not blocked.

"I miss you so much I can't breathe," it read.

It's mid February, still snowing. Now it's two hours instead of one to get close enough to Jonathan to fuck. We ravage one another twice that week. I am a woman scorned and remain furious but he doesn't know that. Outwardly I am pliant, submissive, begging him with every fiber of my being to want me. I tell him about my new therapist and he says he wants to go with me, that he typically cannot relate to therapists, but he trusts if I'm saying good things about her, she could be helpful.

"I can't live without you Jade, but I don't know how to make this work," he says. "I need to keep the company I built from the ground up, and I need Kate to help me run it."

I don't know if I have enough energy left for him, but I do know that I still want him. I want him to choose what WE have built together, and choose it as unequivocally as I have.

The older couple is kind and leaves me alone for the most part. My last night there, I wake up to a familiar yet unbelievable pressure and run to the bathroom, my hands cupped under my crotch. But my hands are no match for the lemon sized clots I leave on the carpet, the bloody breadcrumb trail to the toilet. I climb into the bathtub and watch in horror as my blood streams down the drain. It's been three months since I took the pill that cleansed my body of unwanted tissue. Apparently it wasn't quite done, and I fear I might be dying. I stay in the bathtub until morning.

Around 5am, I hear the woman stirring. I come to, hobble back to my room, and get dressed while staring in horror at the mess I've created. There's no way to hide this, clean this, deal with it, except to face it. I call her in and her eyes widen in horror and concern. She wants me to go to the hospital, and she doesn't even know about the bathtub of blood. She assures me that the carpet is old, claiming they had plans to tear it out that coming spring to replace it. I don't know if I believe her, but I try to appreciate her kindness. I leave despite her insistence that I stay until I'm sure I can drive. There's shame, shame, so much guilt and shame.

On my way back to Kenosha, I call my sister and tell her about the abortion, explaining that my body is not reacting well and I feel very weak. I can tell by her voice how hurt and angry she is. It's painfully clear how terribly disloyal I have been to her. I have betrayed our sister-friend trust, especially with the confidence she had for me to join her at a company she truly respected and loved working for. I have lied to her most egregiously.

She has always had vision-dreams and had called me several months into my affair with Jonathan. She was in a panic from a terrible nightmare she had about me, essentially predicting what was going on, albeit in Picasso-scape analogy fashion. I lied to her then and she no longer trusts me. She assumes I am most likely on a manic run from my bipolar state. I listen to Bastille's "Pompeii" on repeat the rest of the way home and weep; I have no idea where to begin. What is rubble, what is sin?

Mary is compelled to call the head honcho pastor who relays this new development to the rest of the pastoral team. Adulterer, murderer, and unrepentant in one? Oh my! I get a call from David at work. He's weepy and begs me to "save the baby" and "not go through with it." What the-? He had a vasectomy so it's definitely not his and he knows it, but he has found a Christian love for this unborn soul and apparently hasn't bothered to find out what stage I'm at in the ghastly process. I imagine the pastors gathered in a circle, praying fervently for my immortal soul.

My doctor is the elder in the church who saved me from the spider bite. I have nowhere to go but to him. He asks me about the abortion pill and gives me a three-month supply of the specially coated and pricey iron pills. I am a hair's breadth away from needing an infusion, probably do, but the disgust and pity on his face speaks volumes. I take the pills, trying to be grateful for the help, and am once again alone in my journey.

Within days the head pastor calls me again. I don't answer. The voicemail states that I have been found unrepentant and will be publicly excommunicated from the church. He asks me to attend. Uh, no thank you. If I'm not at my own hanging can it actually take place? Apparently the answer is yes because I hear the details of the day repeatedly. My name is bluntly exposed. My adultery is detailed. The fact that I am unrepentant is implied as I'm not there to take the heat. David brings our children to that incriminating service of over 1,000 people, but I am at home with Bon Iver, a wooden, soulless doll determined to stay in my bubble.

The ironic sting of it all is that I have been a secret keeper for so many people in our church. Over the past few years, I had become a non-licenced therapist of sorts who helped a friend search for the secret son she gave away in exchange for her freedom. I laughed and cried with a couple who were not married to one another but kept having sex anyway, and held space for the woman who was covertly planning to leave her loveless marriage. Shall we all be excommunicated together? I understand the pastor's need to make an example of me. In that world, I have as close to a position of authority as a woman can get.

After the excommunication, all help is withdrawn, although my undisclosed friend squeezes in a few more payments for therapy sessions. Sharing a house with David is next to impossible but I have nowhere else to go.

I call my mother and ask her if I can come home to Idaho for a few weeks; I have a longing to walk the rolling hills of the Pacific Northwest and contemplate next steps. She tells me she will not accept me in her home because my place is with my husband.

Knowing how much I've trusted and relied on Jim Wilson in the past, she gives him my phone number. He calls me and tells me to repent of my sins and return to my husband. He asks me for my address so he can send me another copy of his all-too-familiar book, *How to be Free from Bitterness*. I hang up, pricked with guilt for knowing not only will I throw the book in the trash as soon as it arrives, but I plan to cultivate some goddamn anger and resentment as soon as I can get out of my bubble.

People with whom I was once close come by and try to talk sense into me, urging me to reconsider, and apologizing for not seeing my needs sooner.

I also notice that no one directly asks me what happened in my marriage. It's as if they can't see past the picture of perfection we created to be able to discern that there must have been real issues present for me to "suddenly" act out. I am flippant with them in return. Dismissive. Unswayed. I see dismay and disgust on their faces at my flagrant disregard, not only for my soul, but for the life I have built for the last 20 years. How can I just give it away that easily, they wonder. Easy? Nothing about this is easy. But it is literally impossible for me to put my garment back on. If I do, I will die, and I want to live.

One night Allana asks me to take her somewhere special, so we take a mini road trip and go to Chicago. We find adorable restaurants, flirt with the bartenders, and see a play. She takes countless pictures and selfies of us and posts them on Facebook. It's the most relaxed I've been in a long time. I get a glimpse of what my life could look like with the freedom to parent the way I want to parent. One of my dearest friends from Idaho posts a comment, berating me for smiling when I'm in the midst of, "sin so grievous I could lose my eternal soul." I block him. Admonitions are a waste of time. It's March and I see little bits of green emerging from the blanket of snow. Already there's new growth in the torched remains of my life.

My existence takes on a dreamlike quality. One morning as I emerge from the shower, I look at my naked body for the first time in weeks and am shocked. I had always been a curvy, healthy woman with child bearing hips and am now wasted away from longing and severe anemia. I didn't know it was possible for my large boned, 5'7" frame to shrink to a size two. I need to take my health back so I can plan my next steps.

I go to the Y every morning, continue to care for the children during the day, I take my iron pills religiously, and I eat the right foods for my body. At night I find cozy corners in upscale bars and journal while I sip a gin martini straight up with a twist of lemon. I'd always wanted to try martinis. They're sexy and delicious. If I have to be home when David is home, I'm on a mattress I keep in the corner of Sophia's room or watching *Breaking Bad* or *House of Cards* on my computer with earbuds in.

My therapist knows all about Jonathan and agrees to let him come to a session. I was right, he adores her and starts to see her on his own. He wants tight boundaries around our relationship. He wants me to see him and talk to him only when he engages with me first, and I won't have it. I hound him. I will accept nothing less than all or nothing. My therapist quickly falls under his artistic spell. She also plays the piano and agrees that he is incredibly talented. She seems to swoon when she asks me once during a session if Jonathan and I truly take three hours to make love.

I discover that Jonathan is also going to couples therapy with Kate. In my mind, this means he is hedging his bets and I am rage personified. At the same time, my friend can't disobey the church anymore to pay for my sessions, so this is a good excuse to stop seeing my now besotted therapist.

I meet Jonathan in Chicago for dinner, have two martinis on an empty stomach, and begin to demand answers from him. He has none. He equivocates. He won't let me go, but won't let Kate go either. I become enraged and tell him to leave. He immediately stands up and does so. I am left alone at the table, more than half drunk, and realize I have no idea where I've parked my car. It's early March and below freezing with a windchill that takes my breath away. I don't have gloves or a hat. I wander the city streets for over an hour, sobbing, trying to navigate the walking directions on my phone to a place I can't remember, and finally take refuge in a drug store to warm up. The clerk looks at me with alarm but leaves me alone. I call Jonathan. He's on the train over half way home. Fuck him. I call a woman in our care group that I have been close to for years. I thought of her like a mother figure. She answers coldly. I weep into the phone. I tell her I'm lost.

"Well, you'd better find your way Jade," she states, and hangs up.

She's right. It's the kick in the ass I need to hear, so I pull myself together and wipe my tears. I buy a pair of gloves from the clerk. I am not known for my sense of direction on a good day and this is most certainly not a good day. But I want to live, really live, so I am determined to find my goddamn car, and by the time I make it to the parking garage, I'm more than sober enough to drive.

In the meantime I receive the official divorce papers. They must be filled out soon; there's a 120 day waiting period and parenting classes required, and then another wait of six months to a year for processing. David and I fill them out at the kitchen table. I am so relieved he's coming to his senses. I am willing to be the woman scorned. The scapegoat. The issue. The bad guy. I just want my freedom. I've been sitting with my choices and know that no one deserves to be cheated on. I will not "repent and return" but I do ask for David's forgiveness, and I'm ready to make some sacrifices.

I give him the house, even upon sale. I give him the van, paid off, and I take the Honda and accompanying payments. I give him all the contents of the house. I don't ask for alimony. I don't ask for half of what's left of his 401k. He barely makes enough money for us to survive and the kids will need it all. Our parenting plan is 50/50. When I find a place to live, I will take my clothes only. I ask him if he's willing to pay for a room for me to rent and give me three months to start making my own money. He obliges. I have nowhere to go but am determined to get out of that house.

It's late March and Jonathan calls to tell me Kate has discovered his contact with me and has filed for divorce, just as David is finally coming to terms with the fact that we're not together anymore. He even admits he's been flirting with a recently divorced hottie at the gym. His pastoral job is on the line; his house isn't in order thanks to me and the rest of the pastors want him out. He is bitter, but it isn't all directed my way. I take the opportunity to tell him he should reach out to Kate, stating that I know for a fact they would get along well, and that's where the conversation ends.

"That's disgusting," he scoffs. "I'm not interested in a spouse swap."

My journaling in cozy corners started with a lot of longing and pity but quickly changes to needing to figure some shit out. Every bone of my body wants to leave town and start over, but that would mean leaving my children. I try to convince myself they're better off without me. I am so weary. I am exhausted from trying to be a good mother. I've messed up their lives. I've spanked them into submission. I've stolen their fiery light in the name of godliness. I don't deserve them. But reason returns and I mentally slap myself into shape. I am so battle worn and confused that I have to use basic logic and reason to convince myself that my children need me, that I haven't ruined their lives with my past mistakes, nor will I destroy them by uprooting their existence. I have to move forward.

What I do have is about $500 in cash and no solid work history for the past 17 years. I make lists of things I'm good at. Sales. I can sell shit, probably anything. For years I sold the perfect wife and mother routine, not only to myself but to a church full of people. I find a job fair scheduled for sales people right outside Chicago. Now all I need is a resumé and that terrifies me. It can't be blank, nor can it list Pizza Hut and Outback Steakhouse from the late 80's and 90's, save for a recent one year stint at a bean to bar chocolate company.

It occurs to me that I know a couple from our recently deactivated care group that may be able to help if they're willing. David and I have walked with the husband through many past "sins," and he works at a job center helping people write resumés. He is hesitant to disobey the excommunicado decree but I state my case with fierce determination and just a hint of shine. He has me write down everything I've done on a volunteer basis throughout the past 17 years and we craft it into job positions and years worked. In addition to my now non-existent sales job, we've added Event Planner, Public Speaker, Drama Director, and English Tutor to the list. I include Jonathan as a reference and I list the name and number of Rose, the head of the women's ministry at the church. Under Education, I write the two universities I attended, but leave the year I "received my degree" blank, and take a moment to cry for the waste of those years, grieving how close I'd come to obtaining the actual piece of paper and how much it would help me in my job search now. I don't have time to finish my major in Communications and my minor in English. My priority has to be to make a living so I can have a place for me and my babies to live.

None of my clothes fit me, so I splurge on a business casual dress at the Banana Republic outlet, don my trusty black heels, and take my ass to the job fair. It is a sea of desperate people. I'm probably the most desperate but determined not to let it show. Each company has a five minute pitch and then each representative goes and stands behind their booth. I hear promotions for uniform cleaning services, paper products, insurance, and more, but there's only one company I want to entertain: a family-owned fundraising company based out of Ohio, helping mostly music and sports programs in schools make money. It's commission only but there's a draw on future earnings so workers have a steady paycheck. Another major benefit is that in working with schools, employees have the summers off, perfect for a mother with four children. I also know they're looking for only two reps for Illinois, and they haven't even opened in Wisconsin, but this is the most appealing job by far with a well spoken rep named Tim. Naturally it has the longest line afterwards. When it's finally my turn, I smile my shiniest smile at Tim, who happens to be the VP of the company, though I don't know that at the time. All I know is that this job is mine.

One week and two interviews later, I've made it to the last round. At that point, they fly you out to Ohio to meet with the president of the company and a slew of other suits before they take a vote. There is not a single bone in my body that doubts I will have the job, although at the second interview the missing date of my degree was discussed. Of course, they only hire reps with four year degrees. I ask Tim point blank if I've demonstrated a lack of education or intelligence in any way, shape, or form. He admits I'm quite savvy and admires my moxy. He takes me to dinner after the interview and over red wine and gripping conversation, he tells me he'll pass me through.

During dinner I realize with a sinking feeling that the company is staunchly Christian based and, though not required, they prefer "believers." I've already told him of my imminent divorce. I had to work it in after the first interview because I'd received a call from Rose earlier, whose name I had written as a reference. When she called, she had the audacity to lace her tone with pity as she informed me that due to the state of my soul and my untrustworthy behavior, if anyone called her for a recommendation, she would be unable to endorse me. I was frozen in place and said almost nothing. Only when I hung up did I shout a hearty FUCK YOU into the air.

That hurtful phone call can't burst my bubble, though. With every passing day, my light is turning up, up, up, brighter and brighter. Nothing can convince me I won't make it. I already have.

Two weeks later, I fly to Ohio and the job is mine.

To the Outside Girl, with Love

I am infinite source, and I sense the terror behind the triumph.

You know what, my darling?

I am here.

Don't be afraid.

Erase your fear because you have always been, and will always be cared for.

Shame has no place beside me.

You are growing, so this time has not been a loss.

Take one step at a time, trust your intuition.

You don't know it now, but it's your greatest gift.

Your feelings are valid and they matter.

Your voice is powerful and it matters.

Turn your fear into goosebumps of excitement for what is coming.

I am with you.

Don't be afraid.

You are enough and have always been enough.

You are a good mama, and your children love you.

That's a lot. That's enough.

You will always be able to take care of them.

That safe place in the woods by the water is real.

Release control, it's but an illusion.

Be at peace.

Be still and know that I AM and you ARE.

You are already doing it.

You are enough. You have always been enough.

Give your grief to me, I can hold it for you, it's not yours.

Your purpose is hope and light and play and passion.

You are enough.

I will keep saying it until you believe me, my dearest.

VI

How to Begin Again

"Healing is not becoming the best version of yourself, it's letting the worst version of yourself be loved."

11

An Adultress and an Addict Walk Into a Gym...

I get the school fundraising job despite the president's obvious dislike of me and my lifestyle choices. My new boss, yet another man named David, admits as much over the phone, even as he's congratulating me. I'm more "colorful" than their typical rep. Someone my age with my background and history (i.e. church-goer and mother) is typically appealing, but apparently I don't match that description in real life.

I had interviewed for the position just after my 39th birthday and the president had the audacity to question my age. Even worse, several members of the interview panel, all male, asked me personal questions about my marriage and divorce. They don't have an HR department and the patriarchy is booming in Ohio. It feels all too familiar to me and makes my stomach turn, but it's nothing I can't handle.

David informs me that all but the president voted yes and so the job is mine. I'm told I will start in August with training so I can hit the ground running in September. They're going to have me open a territory in Wisconsin, but I "have a lot to prove." No shit, Sherlock.

I seem to be living my own version of Benjamin Button. It's as if I'm shedding years as well as trauma. Apparently my galvanized garment weighed me down just as powerfully as my personal bubble of freedom puts a spring in my step. I am refreshed and renewed, a spring chicken, and I'm constantly mistaken for my children's sibling these days. I'm carded anytime I try to buy alcohol or go into a bar, and then given incredulous looks, winks, or full on congratulations. Audrey and Allana's friends call me a MILF (which I find disturbingly hilarious) and their male friends follow me with longing in their eyes. It's all fine by me. It's about damn time I flaunt a bit. For the first time in my life I don't try to dim my shine.

I'm also incredibly distracted by my newly awakened needs. I'm not seeing or talking to Jonathan, but my body feels so alive I'm afraid I might explode. Enter Christine, a new friend I've connected with through my newfound love for taking care of myself at the gym.

"You need a fuck buddy," pants Christine on the treadmill, running hard with the incline set at 6.

Recently divorced and hysterically funny, Christine teaches piloxing at the Y and has a generous heart under her bossy exterior. She's taken me under her wing and expresses rage on my behalf anytime I tell her what's happening in my life.

"I love me some Jesus," she says, regularly. "I'm not gonna lie, but idiots like your pastor should keep Jesus' name out their mouths."

She makes me laugh and is a breath of fresh air after months of cold shoulders, pity, and disdain from every human I thought I knew.

A friend with benefits, or "fuck buddy" if you're nasty, a thrilling persona I want to explore, is something I've never considered in my entire life. I barely knew such a thing existed. It would certainly be easy to find, especially at the gym. Christine and I belly laugh our way through our weight circuits and attract the eye of every male in the weight room. We certainly have our pick. I flirt with several, even go to dinner and make out with a few, but they are too young for anything more than that. I don't just have an itch to scratch, I have a need to be handled RIGHT. I want to experience something that will help me to keep expanding and savoring my life. I've had unfinished business since puberty. I don't want a boy. I don't want a meathead. I want a man.

I finally find him. He arrives at the Y like clockwork at 10 am every morning, and unlike most men, he doesn't draw attention to himself by surreptitiously watching women, or dart his eyes around to see who's watching while making grunting noises and staring at himself in the mirror too long. His head is bald, clean shaven, so it's hard to tell how old he is. It doesn't matter to me as I won't be needing his services for long; my life is complicated and I have no desire to find a partner. I especially like his gray sweatpants, and like the Jezebel hussy I am, constantly find myself checking out his package. It's quite promising. He wears tight white t-shirts that highlight his tattoos and the prominent veins in his forearms. He smiles at me all the way up to his eyes when we arrive at the water fountain at the same time, which is almost daily by my design, maybe even his as well. One morning he finally asks for my name.

"It's Jade," I tell him.

He repeats my name and gets it right the first time.

"Jade. Nice, like the color of your shirt. I'm Eric." He smiles again and heads back to the machines.

We start to add small talk to our routine. He's quiet, but not shy. There's an easy confidence about him, and I find out he has two sons but no girlfriend or wife. This is important, as I've unequivocally decided to never sleep with a taken man again, to never again cheat or help anyone cheat. I don't need the church's moral code enforced on me to understand how wrong cheating and lying feel in my body.

I announce my decision to Christine, point him out, and receive her stamp of approval: "Ooooweee!" High praise.

Getting Eric to take me out is trickier than I thought it would be. I start by walking up to him at the end of our respective workouts, phone in hand, and ask him point blank if he'll go out with me for a drink.

"Wednesday nights are best," I state confidently. I feel a little like the whole thing is a business transaction; there's a definite end goal and I see no reason to side step.

"Oh! Well, I would love to go out with you, but I don't drink that often, especially during the week."

"Well, I'm sure you can make an exception? I take care of my kids on the weekends, so it's hard for me to get out then."

"Oh. Sure. Well, my shifts start at 2pm and I'm not done with work until 10-10:30."

"Whoa! That's way too late for me. I'm in bed and asleep way before then." What's a girl gotta do to get laid by this guy?

Eric narrows his eyes and chuckles. "So your window of fun is very narrow, huh? So is mine. I'll tell you what, I have a lot of PTO days so I'll take next Wednesday off and we can go out. I'll make sure you're home before 9 so you can get your beauty rest."

Ugh. Fine. I'm asking him out on a Tuesday and was hoping to get some action the very next night, but now I have to wait a whole week. I give him my number anyway and tell him to text me.

About two hours later (an hour and 45 minutes later than I think is reasonable), my phone dings.

"Hey, it's Eric."

"How do I know this is Eric?" I quip, curious to see how he handles small talk.

Immediately a selfie comes through, his lips are pursed, one eye squinted, almost closed, a classic bad boy pose but so obviously put on I laugh out loud. I like this guy. But that's supposed to be beside the point.

The week of build up is fun, more fun than I've ever had just texting someone randomly. One night I ask him what he's really good at and he replies that he loves to draw. Upon request, he sends me several screenshots of his pieces. I'm especially in awe of some of his portraits and ask for the originals they're based on so I can compare. He's spot on. Another true artist. I love artists, and I make the perfect muse.

I gush over his artwork and he throws my question back at me: "Ok, so what are you really good at?"

"Hmmm too many things to list really, so I'm gonna go with massages." I'm sticking with the sultry angle. Plus, it's actually something I enjoy and am good at. "I've been told I give professional level back rubs. I'm the best."

"Damn, I hate to break this to you, but there's only one thing I'm better at than art…and it's massages."

"What? No way. There's just no way you're better than me. That's what we'll start with on Wednesday. I'll meet you at your house and we'll have a massage-off." This is perfect and will get the ball rolling in the right direction. We'll probably be able to skip the drinks and dinner portion all together! "Actually," I continue. "I'm going to need your address. Give it to me and I'll bring you a chocolate shake before you go to work!"

He gives it to me, though hesitantly, and I wonder why, which makes me even more eager to see his place. If it's gross or dirty, not only will the massage-off be canceled, but maybe the entire lay-off. I don't have a place suitable for fuckery to happen, so I need to be comfortable in his space.

When I arrive, I notice his duplex is not in the best part of town, but it is spotlessly clean, beyond tidy, and his bed, king-sized, is made with crisp bedding. He has two extra bedrooms, one for his boys when they're with him, and one that belonged to his roommate who just moved out. I'm pleasantly surprised.

We sit outside on his front steps while he sips his shake, insisting on sharing it with me. Such a gentleman. He's acting shy, a little bashful and uncomfortable which, for some reason, proves to be a turn on for me. I don't need him to like me, I need him to want me. I'm waiting for a kiss, a touch on my arm, something, but he doesn't come near me as he stands up and says he needs to finish getting ready for work, and he'll see me Wednesday.

On the day of our date, I show up promptly at 5pm, more than ready for the massage-off. Eric seems more at ease this time, completely warm and inviting. I make a mental note that he likes to plan things, routine is important to him.

"Let's just go for it!" I say. "You're first."

He smiles at me, takes off his shirt, and lays face down on his bed. I straddle him and give him my best back rub, but I'm a little distracted by the possibilities.

When it's my turn I whip my tank top off, a little sad that I wore a bra, and assume the position. As he rubs my shoulders and neck, which he is indeed very, very good at, I can feel him getting turned on behind me. I have a million butterflies in my stomach and am so wet my pants might slip off by themselves. His hands slide under the top of my jeans. He's still kneading me with his fingers and complimenting me on my toned back muscles. Oh yay, I think, this is definitely going to happen!

Suddenly he removes his hands, slaps my butt lightly, and says, "Let's go get some dinner."

Feeling a bit let down but also still enjoying everything about our interaction, I ask if he wants to go to a neighboring town. I don't want to be seen by anyone I know from the church, and there's a place I really like that Jonathan used to take me. He's familiar with it and says I should drive because he's low on gas, which is slightly annoying to me, but I agree.

On the way, I open up about everything at the forefront of my life and share descriptions of my four children. He's surprised by my age but doesn't make a big deal of it, saying he figured I was in the same ballpark as him, and he's 29. 29 to my newly minted 39...gulp! I push the age difference aside, because again, there's no need to play at being a good match. I'm not and I'm very aware I'm a hot mess, but I'm banking on the hot part.

Dinner is perfection. Light, easy, fun, and saturated with raw desire; the chemistry is tangible. He orders a Captain and Coke, and I request a Hendricks martini, straight up, very little vermouth and a lemon twist, which comes to me in a chilled stainless steel martini glass. He looks at me in awe when I order, which makes me laugh. He takes one look at my cocktail and I offer him a sip. He pushes his own glass away and tells the waitress he too is going to order a grown up drink. I giggle at his phrasing, pleased with having taught him something simply by being authentically, comfortably myself.

We drink martinis and pick at our food. After our plates have been taken away, he finds my leg under the table. He lifts my foot, places it between his legs, slips off my silver ballet flats, and I feel his warm, strong hands rubbing the soles of my feet and finding their way up the wide bottom leg of my jeans to my calf. My huge ass feet are a source of constant embarrassment. I usually try my best to hide them, but everything with Eric feels perfectly natural and right. He never breaks eye contact and draws no attention to what he's doing, sheltered by the long tablecloth. We just keep talking and yearning, and I see the promise in his eyes. We kiss in the parking lot for a while; I enjoy it, but I really just want to skip ahead to the sex part.

Back at his apartment, he turns on early 2000's R&B, music I'm just becoming familiar with and am in full support of the mood it sets. Then we're at the foot of the bed and he's dancing with me, slowly, like we're in a club. He knows how to move, his hips grind as his hands slide to take off my top. I unhook my bra as he removes his t-shirt and the next hour is a blur of want and need.

We start at the bottom of the bed, naked and touching every inch of each other. I've never particularly wanted to have a dick in my mouth, not even Jonathan's, but Eric's is perfect in my hand and I stroke it as he plays with my nipple, flicking and rubbing it between his fingers while he kisses my neck. This alone almost makes me cum and I beg him to fully enter me. He obliges, and the second I feel him thrust into me, a dam breaks and I'm gushing all over his bed. This has happened to me only once before; it grossed David out as he accused me of peeing on him. But here, in this space with Eric, I instinctively know it's the best and most right reaction to his lovemaking skills. I'm everywhere, needing to feel him from every angle. I sit on his face, I slide down his shaft onto his lap and look in his eyes as he moves my hips with his hands. I push his chest and lay him flat so I can get a better purchase and ride him until he groans. Several times I hear him say, with wonder in his voice and almost under his breath, "Goddamn!" like I'm the best thing that's ever happened to him. This stokes my fire even further and I ride wave after wave of pleasure.

Afterwards I feel satiated, like I had been dying of thirst and had finally had my fill, at least for the time being. More than that, I've never felt this safe. Living with David was uncomfortable and awkward at its core, and having sex with Jonathan was dangerous in its exhilaration and demeaning nature, but this Eric guy feels like a solid ass anchor, leaving me free to bob around on the surface and discover things because I know he's got me. I intuitively feel all of this in our first night spent together.

I must be really, really good at choosing fuck buddies. Eric and I are a perfect match. We have sex everywhere, all the time, several times a day, and he is a patient teacher. I need no help on sexual positions, as if I was born with the Kama Sutra emblazoned in my mind, but when I call his dick a penis one day he chokes on his water.

"What did you call it?! Baby, you can't say 'penis.'"

"Okay," I pause, thinking. "Your dick, then. I need you to help teach me how to suck your dick."

"It's a cock." He cups his entire package and thrusts it towards me. "This is a cock. Say it."

"Cock," I whisper, and laugh. "That sounds so dirty."

"It is. It's supposed to be. Sometimes we need to play dirty." He comes close and puts his hand down my pants, fingering my always-wet parts. "And this? This is your pussy." He whispers into my ear, sending shivers like electric shocks straight to where he's touching me. "Damn, you're hot. I didn't even know a woman like you could exist. I look at you and can't imagine where you came from. I can't get enough of your pussy." He sounds tender and loving even as he says words I've never even said in my head. I get that feeling of being anchored again. I'm safe to explore.

"Okay," I breathe, so turned on I can hardly speak. "Baby, show me how to suck your cock right, and then I need you to fuck me. Please. Please fuck me so hard. My pussy is always ready for you." And we're off again. This is my catch up phase; I'm consciously choosing to try things on, to discover what I like. And I like him the most.

We go dancing every weekend that summer. I can get away because nothing gets going until 11pm and my kids are long asleep by then with David available to take over if they wake. I suddenly don't need nearly as much sleep as I used to, energized by my time with Eric. I would stay up all night to stay in this space with him. We are locked in and see and feel only each other as we move to the music.

One night we're taking a breather at the bar, loving the vibe of club Icon, the very same local gay bar David used to pray against every time he drove by calling it Sodom and Gomorrah. Eric takes an unexpected deep breath and then he deflates beside me.

"Jade, I need to tell you something," he says with urgency. I'm all ears.

"There's a guy here that will know me if he sees me. He's a prison guard, and a huge asshole."

"Oh! How do you know him? How do you know he's an asshole prison guard?" I laugh.

Eric looks at me somberly and clears his throat.

"You need to know I was in prison. I'm a felon. I was in for five years."

Whoa. I was not expecting that piece of information to come out of his mouth. It seems so incongruent with the steady, calm energy he exudes. I just look at him, waiting for the rest of the story.

"I was in for theft. But I was stealing to support my addiction."

"Addiction to what?"

"Heroin. I was a heroin addict, there's no sugarcoating it. But I did my time, I've been out for a year, and I'm clean, rebuilding my life, for myself and for my boys."

He holds my gaze steadily. There's no shame on his face, just raw, naked honesty and a vulnerability that makes me want to hug him for a year without stopping. I know next to nothing about addiction or heroin. I've never even smoked a cigarette. I know "sin" and only through the lens of needing a Savior, but this narrow way of thinking about the world has been stripped away, part of my evolution override, and there's not a cell in my body that hesitates at this information. It certainly doesn't affect our friends with benefits status. We are not a couple. And there is nothing that could convince me he's not a safe person.

Over the next several weeks, I ask him a million questions. The world he's left behind is impossible for me to imagine, full of desperation, seedy basements, trap houses, violence, and death. The world I've left behind is equally as confusing to him. It's like we've launched into a brave new world together, and we're all the happier for recognizing no one or anything in that sphere. We're both in awe of our respective corners and spend hours comfortably sharing our perspectives from opposite worlds, finding common ground in the most unlikely places.

Though I have lived in Kenosha for 10 years, there are numerous places I've never been. Eric was born and raised in Kenosha and the same is true for him. I am excommunicated and have no friends, while Eric's determination for a fresh start has led him to steadfastly refuse to stay friends with any of the same people he grew up with. We explore our new-old town together: dancing, live music, restaurants, and bars. We're perfectly content to be alone, but just as willing to meet new people. All I know is that every minute with him feels like fresh air.

Over time, I learn that Eric navigated prison life the same way I've come to know him on the outside: by keeping his head down and minding his own business while exuding an unwavering, steady confidence. His stories of becoming the prison barista to get paid in stamped envelopes and ramen noodles, or playing poker for so many collective years that he knows he could win most tournaments, leave me shaking my head in awe.

On the rare occasions when words fail, when the impossibility of our lives meshing becomes a chasm, we communicate our longing to be understood with our bodies; the tender ferocity of our lovemaking is true and constant. We both have years and years to make up for.

One morning I'm in the bathroom getting ready and teasing him about yet another area in which we're opposite, his body count, which is shockingly high for being in prison for 5 of his 29 years. He comes up behind me, gently grabs my shoulders, and turns me around.

"You know none of that matters to me, right?" he says, earnestly. "Life is short, and there are a million things I want to do. Chasing sex is a waste of energy, but I spent so many years alone that I know I want a partner. Jade, I spent countless hours imagining you. I called you in."

"What does that mean exactly?" I'm used to phrases like "answer to a prayer" but the idea of manifesting your life is completely foreign to me.

"It means that there doesn't have to be separation between your longing and your reality. If you know something is for you, then you just keep walking towards it until it's right in front of you. And here you are."

And here I am. We spend infinite hours imagining what we want our lives to look like in the future and I begin to believe him, to feel the truth of walking towards what I want, knowing it will already be there. It's a journey I've already begun on my own.

Soon after Eric and I start sleeping together, Jonathan starts reaching out again. We text and talk on the phone and I tell him that David's confessed that he and Kate have been emailing back and forth. He doesn't believe me, but checks with her, confirms, and we share a moment of laughter at the accuracy of my prediction. He's giving Kate huge amounts of money in the divorce so she'll be well taken care of and chides me for giving away everything to David so easily.

He sends me chapters of his novel, a novel we used to talk about at length and for which I spent many hours encouraging him. I play a main role, words and acts we've shared are recounted starkly on the page. I feel connected to Jonathan still, not sure I should release him once and for all. Eric has very strong opinions on Jonathan's assholery. He asks me questions as I recount the number of times Jonathan abandoned me when he could have reached out. Jonathan asks to meet me at one of our old haunts and I feel compelled to go and see him; I know I'll understand what to do when we're face to face.

I arrive first and find us a table. When he walks in and sees me, he has a broad grin on his face, nearly running to close the distance between us. I'm reminded of the night I so confidently went towards him only to be turned away. He kisses me. His smell has changed. It's no longer exciting. He tries to kiss me again and I recoil. He assures me that he's mine, that we will figure everything out, but all I want is to be back with Eric, safe in his arms. After that night I find the courage to block him, as he once did me, and fulfill his frequently-stated prediction that his actions would cause him to ultimately lose both Kate and me.

12

Desire Is Your Own Want

It's official: I'm going to move in with Eric and take the place of his roommate. Christine has offered the space in her attic, but I would be taking a bedroom from one of her two boys, and she and her new boyfriend are planning to move in together. So I insist on paying Eric two month's rent, which will get me to the start of my job and a paycheck. I get the promised rent money from David and bring my twin mattress from the house. I set myself up in Eric's extra bedroom, insisting on having my own space and warning him that I don't plan to sleep in bed with him often. I've always thought of myself as someone who dislikes being touched on a regular basis, I don't really care for hugs, and I would definitely rather have my own bed.

It turns out that's yet another story I had been telling myself all along. When it comes to Eric, it's like I'm making up for a lifetime of hugs. From the first night in my new "home," I allow myself to fall asleep in his arms after we've made love and I sleep there, like a baby, all night long. My twin size mattress in the extra bedroom is used for nothing but cunnilingus one sunny morning with R. Kelly's *Cookie* playing in the background. Living with Eric is far too easy and pleasant. I don't have time to worry about how that fact makes me feel, though. I'm still taking care of my children at the house every day and waiting eagerly to start work.

Bright and early one morning at 7am, I get a call and scramble to pick it up when I realize it's my new boss' number. My heart sinks as I listen to his words. It turns out the president of the company just couldn't rest knowing I was voted in as a full fledged sales rep for the company he started 30 years ago from the ground up. He doesn't trust me, plus I don't have my college degree. Did they talk to Rose from the ministry team? I don't think to ask for details as David expresses regret. Everyone feels terrible, blah blah blah.

I'm frozen with fear, terrified and screaming FUCK YOUs at all of those judgemental bastards. If I don't have this job I don't know what I'm going to do. It's literally my lifeline, affording me the ability to strike out on my own. Boss David offers me a chance to prove myself. There are several programs in Indiana, Kentucky, and Iowa sans reps. My job, if I choose to accept it, is to run those programs. I will receive a stipend for travel, be paid by the hour, and receive a hefty bonus if I get the program re-signed for the following year.

I have no choice. I accept. This means I will be traveling for work late August-December for most of the week with the looming threat of having no job at all by Christmas break. My new schedule will be a huge imposition on David who is in the midst of his own crisis and will now be saddled with kids, home, and cooking by himself as he searches for a new job. He's lost his pastoral position, partly because of my actions and the light they shed, but ultimately because he refused to stop seeing Kate.

Again I congratulate myself on my matchmaking skills. Kate's over at the house all the time and they're clearly sleeping together, a fact witnessed by one of the girls. David no longer wants me in the house, the home he's now rebuilding with her. The last time I let myself in the back door without knocking, I see them together in the kitchen, meal prepping, listening to jazz, and sipping whiskey, and I'm told I'm no longer welcome. David has truly chosen the perfect partner as there's no one in the world who will hate and despise me more than he does but Kate. I want to push back - I have no place to mother my children other than the home I was so desperate to sign over to David - but I will be traveling 90% of the time anyway. I double down in my determination to succeed and hand him my key, going all in by going all out.

The next few months are a blur. With little to no training, I am arriving at schools in states I've never been to before, toting hundreds of pounds of supplies around with a dolly in my dresses, suits, and heels, and giving anywhere from three to ten presentations a day. It's my job to get the kids excited and launch the program to the adults, and then field questions throughout the program's duration and keep track of everything via the company's CRM system. I have long hours alone in my car and in my hotel room. I contemplate. I ruminate. I ponder. I have time to myself for the first time in 17 years and I relish it.

As the weeks pass, the results roll in and boss David is elated.

"You're getting signatures and re-signing 100% of every program so far?!" he shouts excitedly over the phone. "Your programs' earnings are up, sometimes as much as 10% compared to last year. What are you doing out there? Whatever it is, keep it up."

How is this a surprise to them? They told me what I needed to do to have a long-term job. I'm going to make sure it gets done.

While I travel, I read and reread beautiful poetry Eric sends me. He's sending me pages and pages of his words that cut through the walls I've built up around me. How could I have found my real person on a hunt for a fuck buddy? A person who is ten years younger than me, and from a completely opposite background? But his words resonate, they are real, and they work like a balm on body, mind, and soul. *You soften my edges while my edges loosen you up. You are the light in my darkness while my darkness is what lights you up....*

I have met Eric's mother, "Mimi," and she's an angel. She was very young when she had him, making her closer to my age than Eric's. She is trustworthy, and Eric had turned over legal guardianship of his boys to her before he faced his prison sentence. She is raising them beautifully. I meet the boys, spend time with them, and take note of the easy, loving way he interacts with his sons. He gets down to their level and is fully in the moment as he plays with them, just hanging out and soaking up every moment being around them. He doesn't waste his time or energy wallowing in guilt or shame, something I instinctively know I have to emulate.

I meet the entire family at one of their frequent family dinners. Eric's aunt is only a few years older than him so they were raised more like siblings. She and her husband have two children: all of the children are all in the same age range as Sophia and Jack, and his Nana hosts the whole shebang as the ever-loving matriarch. The entire family is comprised of extreme foodies. They often choose a country's cuisine and everyone brings a dish to share, the more complicated the better. I am immediately at home. I feel like I've struck gold.

I talk to my kids about meeting Eric and we decide to do it at one of the Sunday dinners. As we get closer to his Nana's, Allana and Sophia start exclaiming about how they used to ride their bikes by this very house and see Nana and her husband sitting outside in their flourishing flower garden. They tell me they had always wished they could see inside the house, to belong to it somehow. My heart swells when they get out of the car and Nana comes rushing to my children with her arms open calling, "Hello my darlings! I'm so happy to meet you!"

The entire night is like a hopeful beginnings montage in a movie. Eric and his boys and my girls play soccer for hours, and we eat amazing food under flickering tiki torches outside in the garden, food that I didn't make alone, while we chat and laugh. Everyone, including Eric's mother and her husband, are beyond welcoming and kind. It's encouraging in a way that's impossible to put into words.

But even when I'm in town, I'm not with the kids very often. Eric's house is not set up for them, and though he keeps it clean, it's high rent and run down. The landlord is a bonafide slumlord, but it was the best he could get with his background check. I start looking for a place and am astounded at the prices to rent a simple one-bedroom. It's all I can afford, even splitting the rent, but I sign a six-month lease and Eric and I move, taking our next steps together.

I'm still battling my shame at this time: both shame at what I've done by cheating, lying, and blowing up my life, and shame that I would do it all again in a millisecond despite seeing how it's breaking my children, each of them affected differently. I am staying in the same town, where I see people I know constantly, people who look at me with pity, judgement, or sheer curiosity to see a fallen woman in the flesh. I hear from a fellow soccer mom that my name was brought up at her backyard barbecue; the gossip isn't even contained to members of the church apparently. She says she shut down the mudslinging, but she wanted me to know things are still being discussed. Eric talks about me to a co-worker and she recognizes my name; she was at the church the morning of my excommunication and warns him I'm a cheater. The see-saw of shame and guilt versus elation and flying freedom is confusing to navigate, and I leave my children with their dad for the most part while I continue to rebuild.

One night, Eric and I are out for martinis and I see the woman from the care group who had collapsed in my lap, Kathy. She is clearly drunk as she sways towards me and starts railing at me about her son, and then dives into what a disgusting whore I am. I am shocked and utterly confused. An image of her son, whom she had been scared of, pops into my mind. I had seen him one of the nights I was out alone with my drink and my journal and we had a casual conversation. I had noticed his avid interest but laughed it off. He messaged me on Facebook shortly thereafter and I invited him to join Eric and myself for dinner at some point, further clarifying my disinterest in anything "more." Needless to say, he didn't take me up on it.

Apparently his one-sided interest made me a whore, and I am frozen in place as she screams at me. Everyone can hear, all eyes are on us. Both Eric and her date are trying to calm her down, and somehow the barbecue soccer mom materializes like a guardian angel. The small town vibes work in my favor this time.

"Leave her alone!" she yells back at Kathy. "You should be ashamed of yourself!" I am confused. I am shaken. I keep my face a mask of composure but inside I am sobbing.

The next day Kathy leaves me a voicemail. She still has my number. She says she doesn't remember saying those things to me, her date had to inform her, but that she is beyond sorry. She doesn't know what came over her. It's another see-saw. I believe I deserve this treatment, perhaps I had given that boy the wrong impression, yet I also have a healthy disdain for the stone throwers.

At work, I'm doing so well running programs in other states that the once wary president relents and they ask me to open Wisconsin as a new territory before the holidays so I can get things rolling. I hear a lot of sales terms thrown about and everything is tracked on a CRM, but to be honest, despite my bravado, I am terrified. I make countless mistakes trying to learn the technology; learning a new system is daunting for me under any circumstance. I've never truly been in corporate sales and don't know what it means to "open a new territory." In practice, it means no one has ever heard of my company or wants me near their schools or programs, an intimidating place to start. Wisconsin's laws are tight when it comes to random reps walking in and wandering their halls. I'm thrown out of schools several times by angry principals and incensed teachers. I have 17 counties to tackle. I know no one, even in my own community.

Boss David rides with me for the first week and emphasizes the importance of belly to belly sales. I have to master the art of the cold call; unless I can get in front of an actual person, I don't have a chance in this business. So I follow the band kids into their early rehearsals before the schools open, or enter as they're leaving at the end of the day. Sometimes I'm up by 3am, driving for hours to arrive at the right time. Presence and composure, a category I've always excelled at, is serving me well, especially when coupled with my people reading skills. I walk through or sign in at the front office like a Jedi, and gain access to the entire school without an appointment. I scour websites to find a teacher's free period, or their Facebook page for personal information, which allows me to show up at the right place at the right time and casually name drop people I've never met.

One day I have five appointments set and scheduled, each of which represents hours of blood, sweat and tears. I wake up the night before vomiting with chills and a high fever, yet I drag myself to every single meeting and sign them all into a program. I'm paying no attention to the data or analytics, I'm just putting my head down and getting it done. I'm often lonely and exhausted, but burning with fierce determination. Boss David calls to let me know the results of my programs exceed all expectations and I'm 200% to my goal, apparently a record of some sort. He promises good things for me at the annual company extravaganza in Ohio.

As it turns out, those good things include being asked to present at a breakout meeting aptly titled, "How to gain access to schools without a set appointment." Read: walk in like you own the place and no one questions you. Later in the week, we're taken to the company picnic at the president's horse ranch, complete with stately barns cushier than my apartment and white picket fences surrounding acres of lush, green fields. No mud fences here! The president is entertaining visitors, and from the looks and sounds of it, he's the bee's knees in the entrepreneurial world with men coming from near and far to hear his sage wisdom. I do my best to avoid the patriarchal bullshit surrounding him like a cloud. Even as I flash a smile in his direction my brain screams *asshole*.

He calls me over unexpectedly and I resist looking behind me to make sure I'm the one being beckoned.

"Here she is in the flesh!" he exclaims, waving his hands Vanna White style in my direction. "The dark horse, the exception to the rule."

This prompts the surrounding men to start peppering me with questions and I field them, keeping it light, while internally searching in my mind for the source, the reason for this entire conversation. I can't help but wonder where this is coming from. As the president keeps talking, it becomes clear: he prides himself on being a good judge of character, on being able to know if someone is a good fit, if they will be successful. He's happy to announce to the growing crowd around us that I, despite being newly divorced with four children, have managed to prove him wrong. His cavalier use of my personal information leaves me frozen in place as he finally asks me a direct question.

"How did you do it?"

"I had to. I had no other choice." My words fall lamely, but they're the only ones I have, so I leave them there and walk away. He thinks he's just graced me with compliments. It doesn't feel like that in my body, but I try to believe it's true.

Because of my schedule and lack of home or funds, I've had my children much less than 50% of the time. I'm already painfully aware of this fact, but David uses it to his advantage one day when he calls me up and demands

I pay him child support. The audacity, along with the impossibility, of the request leaves me shocked and stammering. He says the head honcho pastor recommended as his parting piece of advice that David take me to court and ensure that I pay up, as it was clear to everyone that I'm planning to abandon my children. Au contraire. Despite the pastor's public hanging, backyard barbecue gossip, open attacks, and countless run-ins with church folk's judgemental pity, I've stayed near and dear for my children. I remind him of our legal agreement of 50/50 custody and tell him I'm going to be taking them the full 50% within weeks.

I can confidently drop this declaration because my first bonus is over $5,000, and now I have money to make a home for my children. I've been laser focused on finding an apartment that makes sense and is something I can afford. After infinite phone calls and keeping my eyes peeled, I find it: a three bed, two bath, just blocks from Allana's high school and a mile from Sophia and Jack's school and David's house. I use Facebook Marketplace and a mattress outlet to furnish the kids' rooms. I splurge on little details, like a yellow and pink picture with Steve Jobs' quote, "The people who are crazy enough to think they can change the world are ones who do."

Despite David's ample space, Audrey, newly graduated from high school and planning to be a nurse, begs to move in with me full time while she figures out her nursing school costs and time management. I can't reasonably have her share a room with her six year old brother even with our one week on, one week off custody schedule, so I take the door off the hinges of a large hall closet, hang a curtain, and convince Jack his new "room" makes him as cool as Harry Potter.

Leaving my children with David all these months has taken a greater toll on them than I ever imagined possible. I had convinced myself that I was David's main issue, and that with me gone, his constant crowing about his place in life being the protector of his family, his only real goal that of a role model father, could come to fruition. I know I left him in the worst way possible, and that my apology for the way I left means nothing to him. I know he's drinking more than is good for him, I am too.

My children are collateral damage, shell shocked, traumatized, and trying to make sense of their new world. As the stories roll in, I realize, with a sinking heart, just how much buffering I'd been doing between them and David in the years of our marriage. He has simply switched his abusive behavior from me to them, and they are more vulnerable than ever, unused to his hissing rage and anger being directly levied at them. Still, I continue to take the bulk of the blame. I'm willing to place myself in the middle as the collective bad guy. Plus, David is now engaged to Kate, and her influence softens him. I know he won't act the fool in her presence. Right?

Two things happen that convince me otherwise. The first is feeling inexplicably compelled to join a Facebook group titled, "Support for Survivors of Narcissistic Abuse." I am intimately familiar with the myth of Narcissus, the cautionary tale about the dangers of self-obsession, but I'd never heard that it was a psychiatric condition, a personality disorder. I fall hard down the rabbit hole, sobbing off and on for days as I read post after post of people detailing their lives with their narcissistic spouse, parent, boss, and the toll it has taken, words that hit so close to home that I could practically copy and paste them as my own. I have to sit with the fact that I've been a victim of this disorder, and that I attract it with my empathetic codependence. Although it feels impossible to take on this perspective, I begin to read books and articles to help me digest this information. Even as I label him I recognize that I'm not a professional, that this form of diagnosis holds no real weight, but it's all I have and it gives me something to work with. Besides, how is one to drag their unwilling narcissist to a mental health professional, let alone one that can see past the narcissist's innate abilities to apply charm and twist words to make their partner out to be the issue? That's more than I can fathom.

Allana, especially, has been struggling, just how much I have no idea, but the cracks are beginning to show. When a boy she's been seeing leaks an intimate video of her to the football team, her world is turned upside down and my heart breaks for her. I'm deeply familiar with these fingers of accusation.

Late one night in the middle of a week with her dad, she calls me sobbing and I come immediately to pick her up. She has a suitcase packed and is waiting for me in the driveway. Before she gets in the car, David enfolds her in his arms and says he'll miss her. I immediately sense his dramatic actions and words are disingenuous, and am horrified as she tells me what's been happening. She is the only one of my children able to put it into words. For reasons I'm just beginning to understand, David has always singled her out. There have been several episodes, and he's even shoved her, but he won't show his rage in front of Kate - he waits until she's gone or he has Allana alone in the car.

But the pinnacle of his abuse occurred the night she called me, the night she knew she needed and wanted to move in with me full time. He went down to her bedroom when she was already asleep and woke her up hissing in her ear.

"What do you want to be when you grow up? A cock-sucker? Huh? Is that what you're gonna do? Suck cock for a living?"

I understand from 20 years of living with David and the research I've done into Narcissistic Personality Disorder that I could have tangible video and audio of his actions and words, and he would somehow be able to look me dead in the eyes and deny everything, the classic narcissist's reaction: *"That didn't happen. And if it did, it wasn't that bad. And if it was, it's no big deal. And if it is, it's not my fault. And if it was, I'm not responsible. And if I am...you deserved it."* Since leaving the marriage I have been placating, humble, helpful, even subservient in emails, texts, and conversations. I realize I've been enabling him to continue his treatment of both me and the children. I have years of inbred habits, and my entire pattern of communication needs to change.

To the Outside Girl, with Love

My darling one, you are learning to distinguish man-made God from the Source of all creation.

Slowly but surely you feel the difference in your shell-shocked core.

You are learning the difference between action born of fear, the feeling of I-know-I-should, versus easy flow, passion, and desire.

You experiment with a healthy dose of talking back just to make sure.

There are many moving parts being orchestrated that you cannot see and that's okay.

You are not meant to.

You are an important part of a bigger picture, and you are learning there is no wrong-right-black-white.

There are many parallels happening all at once, and thus your perspective is everything and nothing all at once.

Someday this will bring you comfort.

For now, hand it all to me, your worry and need to know, your desire to will things into existence.

The world does not hang on your decisions, dearest.

You are adorable.

You are all at once powerful, and nothing but a meat suit.

Breathe.

Just breathe.

Take things one step at a time and decide how you want to feel before each segment occurs.

Right now you cannot swim in this ocean, you can only tread water in the truth.

And I AM with you.

VII

It Ain't Over 'Til It's Over

"Instead of asking ourselves what is right or wrong, we must ask ourselves what is true and beautiful?" Glennon Doyle

13

WTF

Through all the family turmoil, Eric stays by my side stubbornly, tenderly, accepting none of my efforts to convince him of my unworthiness. Every time I try to break up with him, he sits down beside me and looks me deep in my eyes, listening to every word, or holds my face in his hands, and begins to gently kiss every square inch aiming, he says, for every freckle as I blubber reasons we shouldn't be pretending we can build an actual life together. I attempt hard boundary after hard boundary, most of them ridiculous and not hard at all.

"You know what I just realized?" I rant one day. "You are younger than the Davidson boys I used to babysit... and I changed the youngest one's DIAPER. I've changed the diapers of humans who are older than you! We cannot stay together longer than five years, otherwise it's just too weird."

"Hey baby?"

"What?!"

"You are so fuckin' sexy, but this insecurity? It's not sexy." I whip my head around, offended, and then laugh at the smile on his face.

There are other boundaries that are much harder to navigate. I refuse to be a step-parent of any kind, and don't want to saddle Eric with that role either. My quiver is full, my plate is loaded, I cannot pretend to be the Brady Bunch, even though together we have the quintessential three boys and three girls to make it happen. With Audrey and Allana living with us full time and Jack still in a closet, there's no permanent place for his boys in our apartment.

All the same, we enjoy being together so much it's contagious. We have every other weekend sleepovers, complete with bonfires, hide and go seek in the dark, movies and popcorn, and play at the park. Our kids get along fairly easily and look forward to every weekend we're all together. Though Eric has taken our relationship seriously from the beginning, never settling for the role of fuck buddy, I cling stubbornly to the façade. I'm aware it's ludicrous, but it helps me feel independent, allowing me to ignore my codependent state. We live in that codependence whether I'd like to admit it or not.

For fun, we recount all the places we've found to have sex in our first three years together: a wigwam in a forest preserve, against a tree in the woods, a swimming pool next to the ocean, the beach, a lake, outside in the rain against the side of the house, even a stolen blow job in a Basilica. We laugh until we cry as we come up with a parody of Dr Seuss' *Oh, the Places You'll Go!* with the slightly rearranged title *Oh, the Places We've Cum!* And I have hardly begun to explore my strange new world, my out of the box possibilities.

Eric is the one who takes me to see the ocean for the first time. Apart from the majestic but unforgiving swells of the Oregon coast, and a few brief hours at the Atlantic from the shores of Baltimore, I've never been anywhere tropical enough to enjoy the water. I haven't been on an airplane but a handful of times. He insists this has to change, that I have to experience the world, and there's no better place to start than the white sand and salty brine of the Gulf of Mexico. He's right. It changes my life. Floating and swimming in the ocean with the sun on my face is second only to being loved by him. How had I gone 39 years without being rocked by the ocean?

After dinner one night we're walking, hand in hand, when I hear Eric give a soft whistle of appreciation. I look at his face in time to see him swivel his neck to see better. There's a look of almost naked lust on his face. Instantly, I tense with a familiar disgust. I knew it! My wall has been up for a reason. I immediately follow his line of sight but there's no hot female across the street, just an old car.

"Damn, she's pretty!" Eric exclaims. "My dad used to have a souped up Caddy like that, a '63 Coupe DeVille. Fuck, I love those cars."

In that instant my last flimsy boundary comes crumbling down. I've been with Eric in every conceivable circumstance and, for some reason, it's in that moment I know without a doubt that his moral compass belies his past mistakes. His code of ethics is something he was born with. Even if I weren't in the picture, I know he would never look at a woman the way he just looked at the Cadillac, he simply has too much respect for himself. More than that, there is a tenderness and compassion he carries for humanity. I found a real man at last.

Eric and I are invited to a bonfire and wander into a backyard of hippies. There's someone standing behind a huge, makeshift iron grill. At first glance, it looks like a young boy in the shadows, but when I say hello a small, elfin-like creature with blonde braids and overalls moves towards me to give me a warm hug. Her name is Heather and she feels like home to me. I'm taken back to Susannah, her son Nathan, and Bill in his teepee, to fine-silt dusty trails and barn cats in the sun.

Being with Heather and her husband, with Eric, and with like minded others, I feel a sense of acceptance and safety. I am supremely comfortable inside my body and beyond, so the first time I'm offered and drop acid is magic. The moon looks so close I know I can touch it, and as I start to give into the sensation, I'm suddenly gripped by fear.

"What if I do it wrong?" I'm now crying, worried. "What if I get this wrong? I don't know how to do this."

Heather's little face looks like a sunbeam as she smiles at me.

"Hey, hey, hey! Just relax. There is no right way. There is no wrong way. It just is. Let it be what it is."

Yes. That is all I can do! It feels like a revelation, a coming home. I carry that feeling with me, and it bleeds into my life. I start to collect experiences that carry the same message; it's the same no matter what I try on. My new comrades laugh at me as I order up these experiences like I'm looking at a menu, but they are always there to provide a safe space, and there's no question in my mind that I'm where I'm supposed to be.

Along with acid, I try mushrooms, MDMA, weed, and coke. Weed makes me feel frozen, and blow turns too many people around me into vacuums of need. But all the others feel like medicine to me. I have always been a collector of words, quotes, and phrases. They find their way to me in this season, echoing like a refrain in my mind: *Everything is temporary, every moment is perfect for my evolution. Let go - I can only control myself. My emotions have a purpose...all of them. Peace is the way, the goal, and the means. Trust and surrender are the only magic pills...*

I want nothing more than to stay in my bubble. I've done the impossible, the hard part. I left. I found a way to make money, to have independence, even buying a car for Audrey and sharing my newfound love of the ocean by taking my children on several epic vacations. Without losing my sense of autonomy, I have accepted Eric's unflappable love. I've revisited my hippie roots and found answers. Now I can rest. But everywhere I go there I am, and there are Davids everywhere.

There's Ex-Husband David and his continued abuse of my children. I have allowed myself the admission that he was and is abusive, and it simultaneously unmoors and empowers me. How can I think of myself as a self confident and proud woman if I stayed in that marriage for 20 years? And yet, as I continue my research and listen to other women's stories on various podcasts, I know how miraculous it is that I started over with nothing. How can I be the weakest and the strongest at the same time? Someone who would cheat and lie, yet show immeasurable fortitude and courage? I don't know how to hold all these truths in my being.

And there's Boss David - every time I talk to him I am reminded just how much anxiety is created in my body when I sneak into schools. In addition, it's impossible to ignore the fact that one's zip code defines the level of education received. Many of the teachers I work with are without proper resources. Though they're spinning too many plates, they have no choice but to fundraise for basic necessities, and it breaks my heart. Those with the least need my services the most, and there's a nagging feeling growing in my chest that I'm exploiting the broken education system to make six figures a year.

Bio Dad David is in the back of my mind; someday I need to find him, to understand my roots. Since I was a little girl I've looked for him in the faces of other men, from strangers watching me from their cars, to men who have inserted themselves into my life with authority and offered protection. In turn, I have unquestioningly accepted their empty efforts, feeling a subconscious need to obey or please them, equating their recognition with self-worth. My "daddy issues" are legion and I need to understand and unravel their impact.

Stepfather David brings to mind the unfinished business I have with his treatment of me, especially around Wes Callihan's abuse in Doug Wilson's self-made denomination. Starting with the question, "How do you know if you've been part of a cult?" I've made myself study the characteristics: charismatic leader, isolation, authoritarianism, fear, exploitation... the list is long and the CREC checks every box. Douglas Wilson is indeed leading a cult and my parents and brother are victims as much as I, a fact which helps me extend empathy, but leaves a million unanswered questions in its wake.

All of these elements have both shaped my choices and continue to haunt me. It has taken over four years to burn down my life and rebuild it from the ground up, but it seems I still have several loose ends.

During my long hours in the car, my frenzied mind tries to sort and contain these thoughts and feelings. I find myself almost missing my galvanized garment - heavy, impossible, but safe. Have I become institutionalized? Since I was a girl, my path has always been laid out for me: who God was, how to feel, how to work, how to parent, how to have sex, how to be a wife, and on and on. But these moments of longing for a dictated life are brief, much like the thick scent of cow shit. When you're nearing a dairy farm, the initial smell is reminiscent of something sweet, like blueberries, then just as quickly, you're hit with the full force of the stench and can't help but retch, your body rejecting the sensation before you even know what's hit you.

To say my relationship with my sister Mary is strained would be putting it mildly. I've apologized to her, tried to explain and reason with her when asked, but she's not having it. I've cut too deeply, betrayed her love and trust. So when she asks a favor from me I jump at the chance. She wants to find her dad and, unlike me, she doesn't even have a first or last name. She has spit in a vial and sent it off to Ancestry.com, so she wants me to do the same which would narrow the results down by half. I'd do a lot more than spit in a tube to continue to repair our relationship, so I do it.

Miraculously, she finds him. He hadn't known of her existence and they begin a mystical reunion. Ironically, I find one of four half sisters on my dad's side. We arrange a time to meet via phone and her twin sister is there, two for the price of one. They were born a few towns over and are 11 months younger than me. The other two half sisters are younger, products of a longtime marriage. When the twins were 16 they met the other two sisters, but no one had a clue I was in the picture at all, except Bio Dad David, who insists on paying for a flight for both Eric and me to meet the entire family at my unknown niece's wedding. I'm just crazy enough to say yes.

On paper this makes no sense and is likely headed for disaster: introducing an unknown sibling to a family wedding, a time already full of stresses and complicated dynamics, seems unwise. Somehow, it's one of the most hilarious, joyful times of my life, and my sisters assure me they share my sentiments. Eric watches us interact, awed by our matching laughs, loud voices, and round, sunflower faces. It's easy to be here with them. I have no interest in initiating a relationship with Dave, but am content to meet him, to hear the family lore, and to join in on the jokes and laughter. The rest of the family good-humouredly teases him, "Hey Dave! How about we put a few more chairs around the table for any other unknown offspring!" I return from the trip willing to learn more about my new family without desperation or need. It's not even close to a resolution but it's a baby step.

I've been fundraising for three years by this time and wrestling with my growing discomfort with the job, both on principle and physically. Even though I've recently purchased my first grown up comfy car, a Buick Regal complete with leather seats and a wood-grained dashboard, the months of countless hours in my small, base model Honda has taken a toll on my body in ways that I'm only beginning to understand. So when I'm recruited by Kraft-Heinz to join a pilot program for their sales team, I apply.

I make it through all the levels of interviews with Kraft-Heinz and sign a contract, but when they ask for a copy of my college degree, stating they only hire reps with a four year degree, I almost lose the job before I start. Just like my long-ago dinner conversation with Tim, I inform the interviewer that I never stated I had a degree, simply listed the universities I attended, and have more than proved my abilities with my extensive resume.

I'm anxious but cheeky because I know in my gut that the job is mine, and magically I find myself with the easiest job of my life, my Heinz gravy train. A work/personal use company car arrives in the parking lot of my apartment with a whopping 13 miles on the odometer. Entering a code to gas up my car versus paying for it myself never gets old. I have an 80k salary with the possibility of bonuses, a whopping six stores within a 50 mile radius (no more commuting through the entire southeast of Wisconsin), and zero cold calling.

When I tell Boss David I'm leaving, he doesn't believe me. To him, it's as if I survived the Oregon Trail, arrived in Wisconsin, cleared the dense trees and underbrush, plowed my field without a mule, planted seeds, harvested just one single healthy crop, and now I'm going to abandon my homestead. I get it. Many of the other reps in the company call and try to talk me out of it. I'm making more money than many of their seasoned sales managers, I've done the hard part, it would be foolish to quit. Yadayadayada. I know in my soul I've created the space in my life I need right now - to heal with room to breathe and ample time spent with my children.

Each one of my children has layers and levels to their trauma. In such a short time they've gone from a helicopter mom with strict rules and a recognizable, regimented life in the church, to feeling abandoned, and now tentatively accepting my regained stability. I can't make it up to them. I know this because my own, complicated relationship with my mom reverberates through it all. I need something to grab onto and find it in a Ram Dass quote: "I can do nothing for you but work on myself...you can do nothing for me but work on yourself." I cannot wallow in guilt, shame, or fear. That will not help my babies thrive in their strange new world.

I need to carefully balance the truths I know about their father with their need to love and feel safe with him. They need to recognize when they don't on their own, and I must be a grounded, calm, logical voice when they need advice. Meanwhile, I am wounded and limping, recognizing how often I'm going to get it wrong. I have a bandwidth that can only reach so far in action.

Audrey, my little firecracker, has been dimmed. She was my first born and received the brunt of my burning desire to be a "godly" mother. Throughout the often chaotic noise of her childhood she's always seemed demure and unperturbed; her intelligence, grace, and kindness has made it difficult for me to see how much she's needed me. I'm just beginning to understand the darkness of her anxiety, the persistence of her emotional and physical exhaustion. So much of this is because of the way I raised her. The road will be long for her to find her way back to herself, but I hold onto the golden tendril of hope that we can re-learn how to be our full selves together. She moves in with a roommate and continues nursing school, which opens us up to put in bunk beds with a trundle for all the boys.

Sitting with my own past has informed me that my little mini-me, my Allana, is simply crying for help. From the outside it looks as if her current landscape is a maelstrom of entitlement and poor choices. She's fueled by trauma, abuse, and confusion as deep as my own. At three years old she would beg to get lost in the woods so she could have a "redrenture." She's made her siblings and me laugh harder than any other human in the world. By the time she was in 4th grade I could give her a grocery list, her own cart, and she would be finished shopping before I was, her head barely above the shopping cart handle as she proudly explained how she found the best prices. I know she needs an adventure to gain perspective. When she graduates from high school, she creates an au pair profile, chooses a family in Australia, and sets off full of hope.

Sophia often demeans me in public for my bad mothering and stupid choices; she is not shy about sharing her distrust of me. I'm beginning to understand how David has singled her out, will often call her his favorite daughter, and I can only imagine what he's been telling her. I swallow both my pride and guilt and continue to ask for forgiveness. I give her physical affection when she'll allow it and simply channel love when she won't. I understand why she doesn't trust me. I am in awe of the power of her young mind to rise above her pain and seek perspective. Of all of my girls, I've worried about her the least because I recognize in her a strength and wisdom that contradicts her age. Every time I show up for her, especially when she hasn't asked for help but I know she needs me, I feel another link of our mother-daughter connection repaired.

Jack's struggles are a whole other ball of wax. He started Kindergarten in the eye of the storm, the middle of the divorce. From the beginning, school has seemed impossible for him to navigate. Collaborating with David through the issues feels unworkable. Eventually Jack is diagnosed with ADHD and even put on meds, but I fight to get him off because they make him even more anxious, and I know that it's not the crux of the issue. What it is, I have no idea, but I need patience and time to figure it out without stifling his being with pharmaceuticals.

Stripped of my fear-driven parenting rule book, I do this all with halting steps and stumbling over mistakes, but it feels more honest, more real, more me. To keep me from the damaging spiral of shame and guilt, I make myself sit with the multitude of things I did beautifully through my 17 years of being a stay-at-home mom. My countless homemade meals and long walks in the woods, hunting for the best swings and pulling my children onto my lap to face me as we sang, "How would you like to go up in a swing, up in the air so blue…." My honest and pure love was always shining through the straightjacket of religion. My favorite part of being a mother was the countless books I'd read to my babies, making sure to change the voice of every character. I would rarely say no when one of my children brought me a towering stack of books and wanted to cuddle in our overstuffed chair.

This helps me reframe the voices of the many "friends" that have continued to warn, threaten, and shame me through the years, telling me that my choices have destroyed my relationship with my children, that it can never be the same. I've even been told anything I did well as a mother is negated by my fall from grace.

Fuck their self-righteous lens. It will be even better. Authentic. More free.

Through it all, I navigate co-parenting with David. He's married, vasectomy reversed, and a new father again, his favorite role. Kate is kind to my children, for which I am thankful. But there have been several other abusive episodes, the likes of which have compelled Eric to write emails to David, human to human, man to man, to call him out. It seems to help when he threatens to expose some specificities of David's behavior to his new church and pastor, but I know there's no way to really stop him; that's not how narcissism works. David's bitterness towards me, his desire to bait me, causes him to use our children as collateral. Sophia and Jack come to me at the beginning of every week, shell-shocked and confused all over again. On paper, David is an excellent father: organized and responsible. He sees me as a hot mess. I can't do anything about it but continue to find myself and show up consistently for my kids.

I savor my weeks without them, however. I feel selfish in my ability to disconnect from their needs and dive into myself, but I know no other way. My new job has decreased my stress levels significantly and gives me time to ponder. What if, for instance, I'm bisexual? I've found several occasions to kiss a girl and I liked it, so what if there's more, for Eric, for me? We have both been products of our circumstances, but isn't every human? Every human is shaped indelibly by family, culture, religion, the education they've received, and the generational chains that stretch seven generations back, seven generations forward; the Bible had it right on this score. Eric and I are always discussing our need to take back our enslaved brains.

So we open ourselves to possibilities we've never considered before and have several beautiful adventures, even a few toothsome threesomes (which turn out to be more trouble than they're worth). First there's Bridget, who becomes more than a little obsessed. Our Scottish friend compares her stalking prowess to Glen Close in *Fatal Attraction,* bantering in his delightful lilt, "I wouldn't plan on getting a pet rabbit anytime soon, Jade." Her behavior triggers Mr. Callihan vibes and I block her with a desperation masked as ferocity. It takes over a year before I'm successful on that front. Another lesson learned.

There's a year-long stint with Patrick. He is a gay, wealthy artist who becomes our friend and sometimes lover. He begins to covet our relationship, mainly Eric's adoration of me, with an intensity and cruelty towards me that leaves us no choice but to cut off contact. There are a few other run-ins with narcissistic red-flag types that make me stop, again and again, to look in the mirror. Everywhere I go, there I am.

"Jade!" I say sternly to my reflection. "This isn't going to stop until you figure your shit out."

14

Operation Re-Parent Self

Enter Astrology. I discover Western Astrology listening to a podcast on one of my many drives. This is not the soft core Astrology of horoscopes, or of a Cosmo article talking about how Aries and a Libra could never work. No, I stumble upon a testimony of a psychologist with a PhD who utilizes this ancient science with her patients. I learn about the history of Astrology, how Benjamin Franklin, for instance, changed the date of the signing of the Declaration of Independence lest it fall on a Full Moon and create an immediate dissonance in the casting of our country's birth chart.

I deep-dive into learning this method. I buy all the books, read the articles, and listen to more podcasts. One day I hear a Debra Silverman interview and look her up. She has an online school and it's expensive, much more than I am comfortable spending on myself. I do it anyway. My job affords me hours every day to tuck away into coffee shops within the proximity of my stores and I study. I print off all my children's charts, Eric's, and mine and spend hours a day using the charts of the humans I know best to understand the intricacies of this science. It's complicated, and in it I find a scaffolding for my gifts of understanding people and what makes them tick. More importantly, I begin to understand myself. Revelations leave me shaken, running to a private place to cry tears of gratitude and sorrow for how long I have berated myself for being who I was made to be.

Studying these charts becomes like a map for my loved ones and for myself that leaves me giddy with excitement. One day I'm sitting with one of my daughter's charts, studying an aspect that helps me make sense of her penchant to use her words as pointed spears. A John Owens quote, often used as a warning in the cult, pops into my mind: "Temptation is like a knife, that may either cut the meat or the throat of a man…" But Owens' perspective seems backwards to me.

It's your particular and unique set of core traits that are the knives, the tools; everyone has a unique set at their disposal. Not one tool needs to be hidden, sharpened (or dulled), or ignored. They're all there for our use, and it's our goddamn choice to pick them up and use them against ourselves, or learn how to wield them and carve out the life we want. How do we uniquely express our traits? What's their impact on others? What is the underlying motivation? The only way to figure it out is to name them, pick them all up, put them to use, make mistakes, and learn without judgement.

I recognize there is a plutonian side of my nature that longs for transformation in my relationships to the people around me, and I'm beginning to understand just how large and unwieldy this energy is. In its lowest form, it kowtows and gives in to inevitable bullies, which only contains me for so long before it builds up to explosive, often reckless and impulsive actions on my part. It's a tool that demands to be used and I want to learn how to wield it in a way that serves me best.

I obnoxiously recite all my learned information to the entire family. One day Sophia stops me mid rant and says, "Mom, if you don't stop talking about my Scorpio Rising next to my Moon and stuck up Uranus I'm going to scream." We all laugh. I try to tone it down but it's difficult. Eric, of course, is the one human who will listen patiently to all my words and, even more importantly, respect what I'm learning and ask questions.

However, with time, even my children recognize the value. I know we've arrived at acceptance when Audrey hands me a piece of paper with a name, birthday, birthplace, and time of birth and says, "Just tell me what to expect with this guy."

Through the years I continue to hear about Doug Wilson's escapades. My mom and stepdad are still part of his cult, my brother now an integral part of his team. In the years since my divorce, I've wanted to remove myself as far as possible, refusing to become involved. My sister Kallie asks me to join a group lobbying to get my old principal and drama director, Tom Garfield, fired for inappropriate behavior towards female students. I steadfastly refuse, pushing away the uncomfortable feeling that, though I often thought of him as a kind protector-savior of sorts, he was not. I remember too many times when his hands were on my shoulders, too many whispers too close to my ear backstage, not to mention his absolute misappropriation of justice upon hearing my truth regarding Wes Callihan. Despite my uninvolvement, he's fired.

There are other horrifying accounts. It comes out that Doug Wilson protected a known pedophile, married him to a 19 year old congregant, and who later had his children removed from his custody when he confessed "inappropriate feelings" towards them.

There's a story made public of Jamin Wight, a boy I was in school with who, as a 23 year old, preyed on and raped a 14 year old girl. Now an adult, she testifies that Doug Wilson's handling of the situation, his protection of the perpetrator, was not only illegal but split her family apart even as he accused her of being culpable because she looked and acted so much older. This one hits particularly close to home. No mud fence, huh? More and more reports come to the surface, but I put my fingers in my ears. I have my own balls to juggle.

Kallie gives my information to a woman who lives in the CREC community and is trying to shed light on these events. I state that I'm uncomfortable sharing anything, that it's in my past. But then she gives me the phone number of a young woman named Emilie and I'm compelled to call her. What she tells me leaves me stunned. When I hang up the phone I am outside myself, gone up to the ceiling, watching and waiting for my body to collapse on the floor and wail with rage and grief. But I don't. I push it down, down, but know if I say nothing, I'll once again use my tools against myself.

It turns out that Emilie is the same age as my own daughter, Audrey. Her math and Bible teacher at Logos was none other than my teacher, the very same Mr. Nance who longed for times past when God's law would allow him to have more than one wife. The same Mr. Nance who patiently sat with me day after day so I could get a C in math. 20 years later, he took another young, bright and fiery girl, spent extra time with her, asked her to be his special assistant, and groomed her. He would hug her, become aroused, touch her breasts. There are far, far too many elements that mirror or match my own experience, including a visit to Doug Wilson's office where she was made to feel like it was her fault. Our stories diverge when I learn Mr. Nance raped her repeatedly over a period of time, but not until she was "of legal age," so prosecuting him becomes impossible.

It took her years to escape the web of lies and confusion but she is now writing her story and speaking publicly about every detail to shed light on this cult that systematically abuses women. The same bullshit is happening over 20 years later. I internalize this to mean I didn't do enough when it happened to me.

Meanwhile we've moved again. Heather has helped us scout a house to rent in a beautiful neighborhood, complete with a wood burning fireplace and giant backyard. It's a bit run down and falling apart, but we are grateful because we have thought it impossible to buy a house. We keep our money separate; Eric has years of back child support from navigating a broken system and running his own business. I make good money, have excellent credit, and have even saved several thousand, but it is far from a buyer's market, and when I start to look for a house and research loans, my hopes are dashed. Not only is my name still on David's exorbitant student loans, but I can't get a first-time, low down payment loan because on paper, I'm a longtime homeowner who should have years of equity.

I swallow my pride and decide to ask David to do the right thing for his children by helping me with a down payment upon the sale of the house. I've done the research and know how much he stands to profit in this market.

"My responsibility is to Kate and my new daughter," he responds, straight to the point.

After the sale of the house, he's able to buy a five bed with a fireplace and an in-ground pool. I fight to look at it from the lens of a lesson, another example of giving my power away to a bully, but there's another side of me that feels I've brought this all on myself.

It's been five years since my divorce was finalized, and every time I've started to feel unmoored, untethered, or overwhelmed I've reached out and Eric has been there. Constant, unchanging, not fire or earth, but air and water, permeable, able to take anything I give him and transmute it. I've become so used to it that when our dynamic begins to shift and diminish, I panic.

It's not that I've seen him solely as my anchor and not as an individual; I've spent much of my time and energy unfolding him, discovering the details, peeling back the layers. It's a delight for me to discover him along the way. I've come to understand how broken the penal system is, how being a felon has left him with a scarlet letter on his chest, a Star of David badge of identity. He has his own heartbreaking traumas and non-traditional parenting of his boys to navigate, and he's doing it beautifully with courage and conviction. He's even figured out how to turn his artistic gifts into a living as a highly sought after tattoo artist.

I can't figure out why he's disappearing when he's right in front of me, where he's going in his head. I become panicked and controlling, demanding answers. I spend a lot of time accusing him of being interested in other women, like the beautiful massage therapist he barters with. After months of this back and forth, he finally admits he's been taking Vicodin. The sorrow in his voice, the dejection I've never heard, the emptiness in his eyes catapults me into a true understanding of opiate addiction. We drink, we occasionally use plant medicine that others would call recreational drugs, but none of these things has made him distant like the opiate Vicodin... He's just gone... I'm probably the only one who can see and feel it. He keeps it under such control, just a few feet away from his normal, that it's almost okay.

But it's not okay with me. In my selfishness, my codependence, I want the vibrant Eric back. The healer in me wants to help him get through it, to the other side, to fight for himself with passion. I have many opinions about how that should look. He listens, he nods his head, he sends me impassioned texts that promise he's fighting for himself, for us, he asks me to be patient. Then I'll catch him in another lie; a lie about where he's getting the Vicodin, how often he's taking it, or how it's affecting him. This cycle repeats over and over.

When Eric first told me he was an addict, my eagerness to throw away the narrow lens of "sin that needs a savior" had been surpassed only by my naivete. Eric has never resembled or matched any descriptions of heroin addicts I have in my mental rolodex. He simply wasn't an addict any longer, right?

I now dive into learning the true nature of addiction, reading and listening to podcasts about this chronic brain disease that alters fundamental neural pathways. When I met Eric he was in remission, just like a cancer patient, but now it's back. The addict in him will lie straight to my face, unable to be honest. My heart is broken for him, for myself. There is no way for me to know how far he'll go, or for how long, or if he'll ever be able to fully come back to me. He's still driving his own car, but his addiction has moved into the passenger seat, pumping a dual-controlled brake, and threatening to take over the wheel.

Eric is the one who helped show me the backwards and destructive nature of shame and guilt and yet I see him returning to it again and again. He's locked inside his own prison where he flogs and shames himself into not taking a pill, does it anyway, and is triggered by the loss of years and meaningful relationships. He's trying so hard, but suffering alone, and it breaks my heart. We weep together, we argue, we sit in silence, and through it all I love him, and want to hug him for a year without stopping.

Through the years I've created my own spiritual rituals. I wake up early to journal, collect quotes as shields, and pull tarot cards like bullets of truth. But when I don't want to, I don't. I don't feel compelled to do anything for the sake of doing it. I'm still discovering the depths and layers of spiritual trauma I have to overcome. I'm easily and horribly triggered. If I hear words like Amen, Hallelujah, Praise God, or the strains of religious music, it sends me into a blind panic. I start going to therapy again.

When my back is against a wall, I organize and categorize. In September of 2019, I make three glorious plans for 2020, one of which is a huge down payment to Debra Silverman's Astrology school. For my 45th birthday in early April, I will fly to Colorado where I will complete the third level of her program, giving me the opportunity to meet her in person and be on track to receive an official certification from her school.

The second plan I put into motion is an agreement to an interview about my experiences with the cult. It's time to take Doug Wilson down.

Lastly, I write myself a letter and set a reminder on my phone to read it on the 1st of January, 2020. In this letter, I sternly remind myself of who I am and how far I've come, that I've learned my lessons and will never give my power away again. I am independent, with an easy job where I make enough money to afford housing on my own. If things don't change with Eric by this date, I will leave. I know I can and I will.

Dear me, you have promised yourself that you will do things differently. Right now you're 95% sure the addiction will win as the most important mistress. But you will not fucking escape, make excuses, or run. You will stay in your own lane and fight your own fight. Your heart feels pretty broken right now, but you will survive. You have changed. You have grown. If you need to leave, you will leave with a plan. You are your own responsibility.

I am finally my own woman. I see my path clearly, I manifest my own destiny, and at long last there is nothing in my way.

To the Outside Girl, with Love

My dearest one, you are going to lose everything and find it again.

I won't tell you of both the pain and pleasure that await you in the coming years.

You would run from one and chase the other, but there's only one way through.

I will be with you always.

You are already enough.

You will forget, but I will be here to remind you.

There's no separation.

None of this, "Now I will do it right. Now I will find myself!"

Don't you know you're already found?

Everywhere you go, there I AM.

And I have enough for everyone.

I am infinite.

Give me your grief, give me the grief of those you love the most.

I can hold it.

Give me your compassion and let me amplify it beyond something merely human.

You will not be lost in the process.

There is no responsibility here.

Give me your unease, your unrest.

You are protected by the same shield every human holds at the ready.

A shield of protection. A shield of love.

Be gracious to those who seem asleep, be gracious to those who seem to have everything.

Their story is none of your concern.

Let me say that again so you hear me.

Their story is none of your business.

Your story is the I AM of your life.

Your story is unfolding perfectly, as it should.

Afterword

Everyone has a story to tell. This is mine, and if you're still with me, you're probably my kind of person, or you can't help peeking through the cracks. Either way, welcome.

Golden Apples, my next book, picks up where this one leaves off. I'd like to say it all wraps up with a tidy bow, but it doesn't. Life just doesn't work that way. Most things don't fit into neat little boxes. We know this. Still, we keep trying.

In this book, you'll hear from Eric. Get ready for some nail-biting, raw honesty, the kind of truth that doesn't require permission. Eric is one of my heroes. And after hearing his story, I have a feeling he might become one of yours too.

A Sample of Eric's Poetry

Portrait

The sensation it gives all the way up my arm, like the most delightful chill a perfect winter day can give.

Fingers exactly where they should be as they caress - back, forth, up and down creating the most intimate feeling between us.

The soft sound and shadow that is cast is just right for the mood of her face.

Slowly my hand meets her face, my fingers touching every shade, crevice, dip and curve.

My body fills with warmth as I see her face very clearly now. It is certainly her, as I knew it always would be.

With a flick of my wrist, a deep breath and a strong exhale, I blow the rubber from the eraser off the paper and the portrait is complete.

Breathe

Feelings of fantasy overcome me
  Past, present, and future, my fingers grasp firmly

Piercing eyes gaze into mine
  Lips locked in embracing adoration

Scents of dark, moist earth explored by few
  Instinctual, primal need arises deep within

Silk touches my lips - her lips made of silk

Pushing deep, searching for a soft place to rest my head
  Sensations of no return

Finally I have landed home
  The overwhelming tenderness of the final fall into bliss

All Within A Breath

Inhale- deep breath, I feel how close it is...
   able to reach out and fucking touch, grab, and hold onto it!

Supported by beams of galvanized steel that have been weathered, beaten, and tested; still
   more than strong enough. With the will of an ant I could support the weight of my mind.

The bridge that promises safe passage every time- much more than a bridge, never ending,
   always enduring.

Across the ocean of treacherous forever!

...Forever

Seemingly anyway. Half FULL is what I always say.
   Attainability is the focus, yes.

She waits at the end of the ocean, the ocean named to persevere: crossed, landed, sandy-white.

Acknowledgments

To Eric- baby, you're such a good sport. Thank you for being endlessly supportive, even when I included intimate scenes and personal details that most people would have run from. You encouraged me to tell the truth anyway, and only flinched a few times (which is honestly impressive). You listen to all my words and have loved me through every version of myself. I can't wait to share more of our story.

To Jess-how many miles have we walked together through the years? A lot. And somehow we still have more to say. I will never take your friendship for granted. Your companionship, wisdom, and laughter help me untangle the hardest knots.

To my therapist, Jen-thank you for asking the kinds of questions that make me pause, squint into the distance, and say, "Damn, that's a good one." For over five years, your thoughtful nudges have encouraged me to reframe the hardest truths.

To my editor, Katie-thank you for being nothing but excited to edit this book. Your enthusiasm gave me confidence in ways you will never know.

To those who backed this self-publishing journey with your time, energy, money, and words of encouragement, thank you. You helped me trust my story was worth telling.

Big thanks to Don-sound producer, music genus, and generous soul, for all the hours you gave to this project. Also, you liking my meatloaf means everything.

And finally to Kaylin- without you, this book would not have made it out into the world. I've never known anyone with such a rare mix of sharp insight, deep compassion, and the ability to do ALL THE THINGS. I'm so lucky to have you in my corner.

About the Author

Born in 1975, Jade was raised in Idaho but now calls the shores of Lake Michigan home. In her tell-all memoir Jade shares her journey as a survivor of abuse and cult involvement, and the messy aftermath of rebuilding her life.

She channels her passion for life into astrology, writing, traveling, and parenting her four (*mostly grown*) children. Jade inspires others to heal, grow and reclaim their power.

Learn more about both Jade and her books on her website.

You can connect with me on:
🌐 https://www.jademari.com

Subscribe to my newsletter:
✉ https://jademari.com/contact